THE MOBILE ACADEMY

mLearning for Higher Education

Clark N. Quinn

JOSSEY-BASS
A Wiley Imprint
www.josseybass.com

Published by Jossey-Bass
A Wiley Imprint

One Montgomery Street, Suite 1200, San Francisco, CA 94104-4594—www.josseybass.com

Jossey-Bass books and products are available through most bookstores. To contact Jossey-Bass directly call our Customer Care Department within the U.S. at 800-956-7739, outside the U.S. at 317-572-3986, or fax 317-572-4002.

Wiley also publishes its books in a variety of electronic formats and by print-on-demand. Not all content that is available in standard print versions of this book may appear or be packaged in all book formats. If you have purchased a version of this book that did not include media that is referenced by or accompanies a standard print version, you may request this media by visiting http://booksupport.wiley.com. For more information about Wiley products, visit us at www.wiley.com.

Figures are reprinted with permission of John Wiley & Sons, Inc.

Library of Congress Cataloging-in-Publication Data

Quinn, Clark N., 1956-
   The mobile academy : mLearning for higher education / Clark N. Quinn.—1st ed.
      p. cm.—(The Jossey-Bass Higher and adult education series)
    Includes bibliographical references and index.
   ISBN 978-1-118-07265-3 (pbk.)
   ISBN 978-1-118-14603-3 (ebk.)
   ISBN 978-1-118-14604-0 (ebk.)
   ISBN 978-1-118-14605-7 (ebk.)
  1. Education, Higher—Computer-assisted instruction. 2. Mobile communication systems in education. I. Title.
   LB2395.7.Q56 2012
   378.1′7344678—dc23

                                                2011030031

Printed in the United States of America
first edition

PB Printing 10 9 8 7 6 5 4 3 2 1

Contents

List of Figures

Foreword

When venturing into uncharted space, it's always good to have a guide. Even when looking in your own backyard, having an astute observer with you can point out things you never focused on before. So, when exploring the mobile academy you could not find a better guide than Clark Quinn. We are clearly at a critical juncture when it comes to mobility and mobile learning.

Reports such as the *National Broadband Plan* and the *National Educational Technology Plan* highlight the need to effectively use communications technology and mobility in all segments of our lives, but especially in education.

Reports such as the *Horizon Report* and organizations such as EDUCAUSE and other leadership groups point to transformational change that is beginning to occur. How you put this in context, evaluate, and plan for this coming sea change will determine the course of education, and no one has done more research or thinking about these issues than Clark Quinn.

I first met Clark more than thirty years ago when we were both at DesignWare. He was a recent college graduate and was developing educational software for a new tool—the personal computer. At that point in the 1980s, the personal computer was just beginning to move from the lab to schools and ultimately to homes. Following his time at DesignWare, he went on to earn a Masters degree and a Ph.D. He has taught both at universities here and abroad, as well as worked in the field of corporate training. He is recognized as an expert in this area and is widely sought as a consultant by both educators and industry leaders. He brings his wealth of experience and insight to *The Mobile Academy*. It is the way of the future, and having such a book at your fingertips can only help you make the right choices as you move forward to offer your students the best education possible.

John C. Ittelson

To my dear wife, LeAnn, who has shared, supported,

and endured my postgraduate endeavors

Preface

There's a fundamental revolution being sparked by the advent of ubiquitous mobile devices. The devices are everywhere, and they are enabling changes in society (communications supporting revolutions), commerce (paying with your phone), and interpersonal relationships (sexting!). The very omnipresence of these devices also suggests a change in education, and the question really is whether it is something that happens or something we take advantage of.

In short, we have new power in our hands, and we can use it for good or ill. To use mobile for good, and in particular for learning, we need to understand the power on tap, look at some principles and examples, and get going.

AUDIENCE

This book is for the higher education instructor and the folks that support them as instructional designers or in administrative services. This book provides guidance for the applications of mobile learning to support the student learning experience, which includes meeting administrative needs of the learners, but mostly focuses on facilitating learning.

GOALS

This book provides the background information necessary to successfully design mobile learning solutions. This book provides you with a background in mobile devices and platforms and a model for mobile learning. It also includes practical advice and examples on implementing mobile for:

- Administrative needs
- Support for content delivery
- Delivery of meaningful practice
- Adding the value of social learning
- A look at what's coming
- Organizational and implementation issues

The goal is to help you consider how mobile can improve the learner experience, making the higher education process both easier and more effective, and to support you in taking advantage of the opportunity.

STRUCTURE

This book starts with an overview that documents why it is time to talk *mobile*. Following are two foundation chapters covering mobile devices and learning, to provide common ground for the ensuing discussion.

The core of the discussion is laid across four chapters and starts with the administrative ways mobile can facilitate the learner experience. The core of the learning experience is then broken into components: the content around the learner activity; the meaningful tasks or practice in which the learner engages; and social learning.

The book concludes with a look toward the future, some practical issues of implementing mobile in an organization, and encouragement to get going.

RECOMMENDATIONS

This book was written with an expectation that you will read it in order. Instructors and course designers may be able to jump straight to Chapter Five and proceed, if you are familiar enough with both mobile devices and pedagogy and want to begin looking for ideas to augment your classes. I expect administrators to be more concerned with Chapters Four and Nine.

Acknowledgments

As with my previous efforts, I am indebted to many who have supported me in this initiative. My family is first, including my wife, LeAnn, my son, Declan, and daughter, Erin, who have put up with my heavy workload and consequent seclusion in my dungeon. Also, my mother, Esther, and brother, Clif (and indirectly his family), have never wavered in their support.

Academically, I am very fortunate to have been supported by my undergraduate advisers Hugh Mehan and Jim Levin, thesis supervisor Donald Norman, postdoctoral supervisor Leona Schauble, head of school Paul Compton, and colleague John Ittelson, as at least a partial list. They gave me space to learn and the necessary guidance to succeed.

My nonacademic career mentors include Jim Schuyler, Ron Watts, Rim Keris, Joe Miller, Charlie Gillette, and Mohit Bhargava, all of whom have taught me valuable lessons. Carmel Myers and Ken Majer bridged academia and career, mentoring me within campus administration. My colleagues in the Internet Time Alliance—Jay Cross, Jane Hart, Harold Jarche, and Charles Jennings—have served as collaborators in social learning and have provided both valuable insight and much support.

Erin Null has been my acquisition editor and provided me this opportunity and valuable feedback. Cathy Mallon, as my production editor, has been flexible yet firm. Thanks to John Traxler, Grant Beever, and Alan Levine, who all kindly gave me time and assistance. A second thanks goes to John Ittelson for agreeing to write the foreword.

To all those and the many more who have played a role, I give my fervent thanks and grateful appreciation.

About the Author

Clark Quinn leads learning system design through Quinnovation, providing strategic solutions to Fortune 500, education, government, and not-for-profit organizations. Previously, he headed research and development efforts for Knowledge Universe Interactive Studio, and before that he held executive positions at Open Net and Access CMC, two Australian initiatives in internet-based multimedia and education. Clark is an internationally recognized scholar in the field of learning technology with an extensive publication and presentation record and has held positions at the University of New South Wales, the University of Pittsburgh's Learning Research and Development Center, and San Diego State University's Center for Research in Mathematics and Science Education. Clark earned a PhD in cognitive psychology from the University of California, San Diego, after working for DesignWare, an early educational software company. An early innovator, Clark was part of a project conducting learning discussion via e-mail in 1979 and has maintained a consistent track record of advanced uses of technology including mobile, performance support, intelligently adaptive learning systems, and award-winning online content, educational computer games, and web sites. He is in demand as a speaker both nationally and internationally and has published *Engaging Learning: Designing e-Learning Simulation Games* (Pfeiffer, 2005) and *Designing mLearning: Tapping into the Mobile Revolution for Organizational Performance* (Pfeiffer, 2011), as well as numerous articles and book chapters.

THE MOBILE ACADEMY

The Mobile Revolution

The mobile revolution is truly here. For example, in the case of mobile phones, the odds of finding someone who doesn't own one are close to zero. Cell phones aren't the only mobile device, but they are a growth area because increasingly they include the capabilities of other mobile devices. However, tablets are also on the rise, cannibalizing laptop sales (The Street, 2011). Particularly in the academy, the greatest ownership of mobile devices is in the traditional-aged college student demographic: The Pew Internet February 2010 report points out that adults younger than 30 are more likely to own a cell phone, at an ownership rate of 93% compared with 83% for all adults over 18.

CONTEXT

Globally, access to mobile networks is now available to 90% of the world population, according to the "World in 2010" report put out by the International Telecommunications Union (ITU). Perhaps most importantly, the same ITU report details that the developed world mobile market is reaching saturation, with 116 subscriptions for every 100 eligible individuals. And, unlike laptops, you can't prevent access by shutting down a wireless network; access is now everywhere you get a cell phone signal. Consequently, the question is not whether to allow internet access but how to accommodate it.

Yet campuses have been slow to adapt to the mobilized student. The 2010 Campus Computing survey shows that only 13.1% of institutions already have developed or enabled mobile learning and administrative capabilities, and only another 10.1% are doing so in the 2010–2011 academic year.

The discrepancy between distribution of mobile devices and university uptake likely has several factors, including:

- The relative newness of what David Pogue, New York Times technology writer, calls *app phones*, which not only have internet access but also can host different local software applications
- A turbulent marketplace
- Vendor slowness to invest in what is a relatively new market in tough economic conditions

The ability of phones to provide custom learning solutions is a recent development. While there have been a variety of services delivered, and learning needs met, via text messaging elsewhere, the use of text messaging has been slower to penetrate the U.S. market, and other mechanisms are even more limited. Consequently, the opportunity to provide richer interactions is still emerging.

The marketplace on which to develop those richer interactions has remained unstable. At the time of writing, one of the major players a few years ago, Palm, has essentially disappeared, though the operating system it developed for the next generation may yet achieve success in new hands.

While the platform operating systems are finally seeing some stability, the hardware and marketplace are still in a state of almost constant change, which makes it hard to determine a successful strategy. As a consequence, vendors of tools and technologies have been slow to invest in the development of mobile capabilities.

Yet we now have achieved a state of sufficient stability to start building mobile solutions, and the dynamism that prevented investment is now being exhibited in the market that capitalizes on that investment. Further, the devices also provide internet access, to the point that, for many, mobile is the main form of internet access (OnDevice, 2011).

This leads to our topic: the opportunity and the future, specifically around higher education learning. Mobile has matured and stabilized to the point where it now makes sense to understand, plan, and start developing mobile solutions. There are already predictions that mobile will fundamentally alter the delivery of learning. With ubiquitous access, why would learning continue to be tied to a location or a time? What we have on tap is the opportunity to revisit the fundamentals of the learning experience and use technology to come closer to the ideals we would like to achieve.

The real opportunity here is to facilitate deeper and more persistent learning. In an all-too apt skit, comedian Father Guido Sarducci talks about the five-minute University: "The idea is that in five minutes you learn what the average college graduate remembers five years after he or she is out of school" (http://www.youtube.com/watch?v=kO8x8eoU3L4). The point is that too much of education in general has been tied to industrial efficiency instead of learning effectiveness. As Long and Holeton (2009) point out, the aim was to prepare individuals to be useful factory employees performing repetitive tasks. The classroom model was developed to accommodate the ability to serve a number of students instead of the more inefficient apprenticeship model, and the focus was not on ensuring competency but on finding who would succeed. More fundamentally, what we learn in our college experience is of little use in our everyday lives. And, as Professor Emeritus John Ittelson says, universities are good at resisting disruption from new technologies. Our investment in education disappears too soon after the event. We need to revisit learning. Mobile is not a cure but is a tool to achieve the ends, and consequently it is a catalyst for change.

I believe that technology has been such a catalyst. Arthur C. Clarke said with much foresight, "Any sufficiently advanced technology is indistinguishable from magic" (1984). We really have reached the point where we do have magic, and thus we have the opportunity to ask what we should do with it. When we went back and looked at what makes good learning, to see how to use technology, I think we recoiled in shock from what we were doing in the classroom. So I will characterize effective learning as part of discussing how mobile can be used to facilitate it.

RELATED EXPERIENCES

The use of mobile devices is growing in other arenas. In the corporate market, where productivity improvement opportunities are quickly capitalized on, mobile is finally on the upswing. Examples range from training courses on phones through performance support and information access capabilities to augmented reality games to build teams and enhance learning. While academic research continues to lead in concepts, the corporate sector tends to move quicker on practical application and larger-scale innovation. They are also more focused on outcomes.

K–12 education, too, is seeing growing use of mobile. From Elliot Soloway's pioneering work with PDAs for kids (Soloway et al., 1999), collecting data via sensors and uploading, we have seen uses of mobile devices extend from e-books and clickers (audience response systems) for data collection to communication and location-based activities and more. K–12 education has different demands in terms of learner developmental level, ubiquity of devices, and institutional inflexibility, but the goal of formal education is shared.

Around the world, mobile devices have become a tool for empowerment. Farmers have been able to access information about crop prices and free themselves from the tyranny of a single buyer. Health information about safe sex made accessible on cell phones in Africa has the potential to save lives.

Mobile is also changing behaviors. When shoppers are reported going alone into changing rooms but staying longer, it turns out that they are taking pictures of themselves in their selections and sharing with their friends to get opinions. Actually turning off a cell phone during a conversation signals the importance of the discussion. And, tragically, individuals are feeling the need for communication so drastically that they are willing to risk their lives to drive while texting.

Mobile activities across domains inform the discussion but do not define it. While we can learn from what they have achieved, we need to abstract the principles and recontextualize them for the purposes of learning in higher education. We are seeking a path that uniquely characterizes what we can do in the academy to facilitate learning.

WHY HIGHER EDUCATION NEEDS TO PAY ATTENTION

Higher education does need to pay attention to the opportunities others are seizing and the societal changes that are occurring. Mobile devices are out there, and consequently they can be ignored to the instructor's peril or capitalized on for the learner's benefit. Students may be tweeting about the class, for instance, or in response to questions or issues in the class. They could be using their phones to send text messages or to answer questions posed by the instructor.

A number of years ago, I visited a higher learning institution that had installed high-tech classrooms. They had cameras, projectors, and wireless Internet. At the time, the faculty were asking that the Internet be disabled because they were afraid that the learners might be surfing or, of all horrors, day-trading. At the time, my thought was, "You can lead a learner to learning, but you can't make them think" (paraphrasing Dorothy Parker); if you cut off the Internet, students could still play solitaire. If you took away the laptops, they could still doodle. In short, you cannot force learners to pay attention; they will vote with their eyeballs and ears, and you better have a compelling value proposition.

Today, things are even worse from this perspective. You can't control learners' mobile devices, which increasingly have internet access. There are two sides to the issue of internet access, as suggested already, but the increasing power of connectivity exacerbates the situation. On the negative side, learners not only can distract themselves but also can interact with others. With social networking tools like Twitter and Facebook, they can be having a side conversation, even about the subject matter and the instructor. This has already happened at a conference, where a speaker was pilloried by tweets from audience members and the awareness was shared broadly.

The upside, however, is worth considering. In Jane Bozarth's (2010) prescient book *Social Media for Trainers*, she touts a wide variety of ways to use social media in the training room, and this extends to the classroom. Beyond social, further opportunities also exist to extend the university experience to enhance learning, student satisfaction, and of course those derivative outcomes: recruitment, retention, and completion. The opportunities include tools, content, interactions, and more.

The inherent nature of mobile devices has been quick and contextual access (Palm, 2003). This is changing with tablets supporting more prolonged experiences, and greater support for learning as opposed to information access. These are topics we will explore.

THE REST OF THIS BOOK

This book, as suggested, is about ways to use mobile to improve and optimize the learner experience. The mobile field is incredibly dynamic, as a new area tends to be. While some principles are emerging, the pragmatics change almost daily.

So, while I can talk about solutions, I can't talk about implementation in any meaningful way that won't be out of date before the book is available in print. As such, throughout the book I discuss principles and concepts rather than the specifics of implementation such as coding and tools. Where opportunities exist, I mention approaches to implementation, but that is not the focus. After all, if you get the design right, there are lots of ways to implement it; if you don't get the design right, it doesn't matter how you implement it.

Outline of What Is to Come

To truly capitalize on the opportunities for mobile devices to improve the learning experience, two essential background components are an understanding of mobile devices, covered in Chapter Two, and an understanding of good learning, discussed in Chapter Three.

From there, the components of the learning experience are broken down. Chapter Four considers the context of learning, including the institutional setting and administrative functions.

The various functions of learning are then examined in Chapter Five on content delivery, Chapter Six on the opportunities for interactive learning, and Chapter Seven on social learning.

Chapter Eight tackles topics that are on the horizon, including augmented and alternate reality, adaptive systems, and meta-learning. Chapter Nine looks at the organizational issues including platforms and policies before giving a call to action.

PRACTICE

1. Investigate the platforms currently in use on your campus: Which have mobile options already available? Are any enabled at your site?

2. What can you find out about your institution's population and their device profiles? Does this information already exist? How could it be collected?

2

Foundations: Mobile

To take full advantage of mobile technology, it helps to get a handle on just what mobile is (and is not). This chapter reviews mobile learning to establish a definition and outlines mobile devices and technologies. The goal is to create a shared understanding that will ground the subsequent discussions.

DEVICES

It is necessary to briefly characterize the devices. A more comprehensive treatment can be found in my previous book on mobile, *Designing mLearning: Tapping into the Mobile Revolution for Organizational Performance* (2011), and an exhaustively researched history appears in Gary Woodill's *The Mobile Learning Edge: Tools and Technologies for Developing Your Teams* (2010). A brief characterization suggests that the market is converging as devices are increasingly integrating a rich set of capabilities.

Portable phones arose at roughly the same time as the first attempts at portable computers: In the late 1970s initial efforts were made, and useful, truly pocketable editions arose in the mid-1990s. The PDA took off when Palm successfully developed its handhelds. The first smartphones arrived in the late 90s, but it was in 2001 and 2002 that phones incorporated Palm's software, Microsoft released its Windows Mobile software, and the Blackberry from RIM emerged.

Other mobile devices were later to the game. Digital media players were clunky or hard to use until Apple's iPod was released in 2001. While Nintendo's Game

Boy had enjoyed success throughout the 90s, the release of the Nintendo DS (Dual Screen) in 2004 really sparked the notion of a handheld gaming *platform*, complemented the same year by Sony releasing the PlayStation Portable (PSP).

While there are still cell phones separate from smartphones (though the sales of smartphones are predicted to outpace cell phones as of Q3 2011; Nielsen, 2010) and some PDAs are still in use alone or coupled with a cell phone (and there are game platforms or media players), the web-enabled phone is almost ubiquitous these days, at least in the developed world. Almost all cell phones available today have browsers, though the owners may not know it or have data access enabled. So the easy way to think about devices is as an abstraction from the smartphone.

Tablets are a divergence, as they typically do not have cell phone voice technologies but can get data through wireless phone networks or through wi-fi in other cases. They can use a Voice over Internet Protocol (VoIP), however, so voice is not completely precluded (more below). I used to believe that from the point of view of mobile devices, a tablet is not much different from a smartphone in capabilities and consequently in planning and design, but my view is changing.

As tablets converge on a form factor roughly book sized, the greater screen area means tablets can support rich media consumption and consequently can support deep engagement. Touch screens and more intimate viewing positions makes the experience on a tablet fundamentally different from that on a laptop at arm's length, but the tablet's size is less mobile and less likely to always be with the individual, changing the nature of the interaction. Tablets may make more sense than mobile devices to use for formal learning. Particularly when it becomes easy to develop cross-platform solutions that go beyond just media playing to support rich interaction both programmatic and social, the potential of tablets to support learning is likely to be very high.

The form factor, however, is appealing, and as of this writing 65 or 80% of Fortune 100 companies either have already deployed iPads or are piloting their use (TUAW, 2011). Consequently, tablets likely will make sense if they are provided or required but are not yet to be assumed to be with everyone everywhere, unlike mobile phones.

The convergent model (Figure 2.1) is of a device that:

- Has a processor and memory onboard
- Has an operating system

- Supports a suite of supplied or customized applications (apps) to run
- Provides a way for the device to communicate to the user, whether audio, screen, or vibration (or all of the above)
- Has a way for the user to communicate to the device, whether audio, touch screen, physical inputs, or a combination
- Possesses a way for the device to communicate to the digital world, whether through mobile phone networks, wireless Internet (i.e., wi-fi), or occasional synchronization via cables
- Frequently has ways for the device to sense the ambient environment such as with camera, microphone, or global positioning system (GPS)

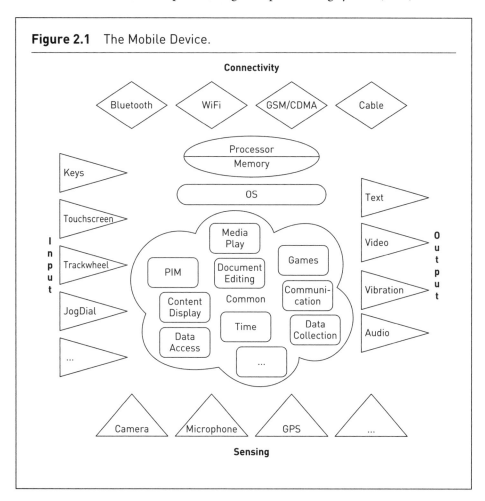

Figure 2.1 The Mobile Device.

Given the characteristic pattern of use previously identified, quick access many times, the requirement for instant on, and high reliability have been historically important components of mobile devices as well.

Another benefit of an integrated device is the ability to share information between applications. I finally got a smartphone when I was tired of looking up a phone number in my PDA and typing it into my cell phone. Similarly, cutting data found on a web search and pasting it into a communication or taking an e-mail address from a communication and putting it into an address book, all to be seamlessly synched with the desktop, is an effectiveness boost.

These characteristics describe essentially all mobile devices out there and provide a consistent basis for thinking about mobile learning for the academy. At the core, these devices are platforms that use a processor coupled with memory running an operating system in a mobile form factor. There have to be sensors and input devices that allow the device to communicate with the user, and there must be connection capabilities that allow the processor to connect to the rest of the digital world, whether continuously or intermittently.

These devices can differ on a variety of dimensions:

- They can take a wide variety of form factors (e.g., phone, PDA, tablet).
- They can have a variety of different ways to communicate with the digital world and with users.
- They may incorporate a variety of ways of sensing the nondigital world.

While all of them have a portable processor and communicate with the digital world and the user, it is worth understanding their variables to explore which mobile solutions might be available and useful in learning.

Output

The first way these devices can differ is how they communicate with the user. Main mechanisms are visual, auditory, and *haptic* (the term for physical feedback). The goal is to communicate to the user information the user is looking for. This can be analog or semantic and continual or discrete.

Screens are a common way devices communicate with user. From limited black-and-white screens, we have moved to screen resolutions that begin to approach those seen first on desktops, with color and screen sizes capable of showing movies. Screens tap into our powerful visual processing system.

Projection is a new, and rare, capability, where devices not only can present on screen but also actually can beam the image onto a nearby surface, which facilitates sharing the output. While generally personal, mobile devices can be shared (I personally keep diagrams and screenshots on my device to share in problem solving).

Lights are another way devices can communicate. They can change color, can flash, or can simply toggle between on and off depending on status. While not a rich media, they can provide status information.

Speakers are a way devices can communicate via audio. As mentioned earlier, audio is nondirectional and can carry speech as well as sounds.

Earphones are essentially the same as speakers but are private rather than shared.

Haptic communication is a tactile category, where the output comes from physical movement. A familiar mechanism is vibration. Though it may seem inconsequential, the physical feedback (the *touch* of a keyboard) has been important to people. Ted Selker, while at IBM, demonstrated a laptop whose pointing device provided a distinctive bump feel as you rolled over a window boundary. More such feedback may appear in the future.

Input

There are also a variety of ways we can provide input to a device, mostly centered on digital, which in this case means via fingers not binary data. Input typically must communicate a selection between options, indicate a changing state, or specify a point along one dimension or two (such as screen location). A variety of devices have evolved to variously support these needs.

Touch screens were the earliest form of input on PDAs, though often accomplished with a stylus. Advances in sensing and user interface (UI) have allowed fingers to be effectively accurate pointers as well. Note that touch screens can represent many familiar hardware devices, notably buttons, keypads, and keyboards, but use touch sensitivity rather than dedicated mechanics.

Buttons are a simple form of input that signal a state change or, when held according to a time function usually with visual feedback, can indicate a point on a continuum. Coupled with visual cues, *soft* buttons can also convey different meanings in different contexts, unlike *fixed* buttons with specific purposes (like on–off buttons). Another example is the familiar mobile phone keys often seen accompanying the numeric keypad, with left, right, up down, and center buttons.

Keypads are arrays of buttons for specialized functions. They can be specialized, and familiar layouts are used in various circumstances, for instance, the 10-key arrangement, which can be used for phone numbers or for numeric data (with different layouts, oddly).

Keyboards are keypads specifically for textual input, though often they also support other buttons and keypads.

Track wheels or jog dials are input devices with a round wheel (as on the iPod) that uses rotary motion to map to a continuum of values (so, for instance, rolling left turns down volume; rolling right turns it up). They often can work in other dedicated roles as well, serving for example as buttons for up, down, forward, and back.

Trackball is a device that allows one-dimensional and two-dimensional specifications. Some also support pushing as a button.

Accelerometers are small instruments that can detect movement, providing a new way for users to communicate to their devices. By shaking or turning a device, users can signal an action. Additional sensors are being developed to detect other user-generated changes.

Voice is also sometimes a control option, and voice recognition is getting more powerful all the time and can work not only for direct commands but as a text-entry mechanism as well.

While capabilities in input haven't changed significantly and most changes are liable to be evolutionary instead of revolutionary, the continuing miniaturization of technology and increasing capability of devices means the input possibilities like will continue to expand. By being able to communicate with (and through) the devices, we are delivering mobile processing and consequently augmentation capabilities.

Sensors

Mobile devices do not have to be totally dependent on user input to understand what context they are in. Microcircuits have been developed that can take a wide variety of information from their environment.

A *global positioning system* (GPS) is a geolocation approach that triangulates position using a set of orbiting satellites with known locations. Originally used by the military, this system has now been made available for civilian uses. While there are dedicated systems for location, this capability is now being made available in more general mobile devices.

Cameras are now in many mobile devices as well. Capable of still or video capture, they can also stream the camera image to the screen, with additional information laid on. There are increasing forms of visual data encoding (e.g., bar codes, quick-response [QR] codes) that will support attaching device-readable data to the ambient environment, allowing a location to provide information to the user.

Radio frequency identification (RFID) is a technology that allows devices to read signals from a proximal object (typically, they can be inserted in animals or even people). Business use, though not widespread, includes taking inventory. For instance, Walmart required its top suppliers to tag all merchandise with RFID tags.

Microphones allow devices to hear what is available in the environment as ambient information and to record audio. A second microphone can be present, to detect and be used to cancel out ambient noise.

Compass capabilities allow devices to know which way they are facing. This information can be productively coupled with GPS systems to provide more location data and to support augmented reality.

Accelerometers not only are used for input from the user but potentially also can provide information about the user's movements in the broader context.

The adding of sensors is an area that is still being explored, with new ones regularly being announced in forthcoming devices. For example, the Motorola Xoom has a barometric pressure sensor, and a thermometer is not hard to imagine. Some PDAs had an easy way of adding external inputs via hardware sockets, and special ones are being made with specific characteristics for dedicated purposes; however, more opportunities will arise. It may be possible to add medical information such as blood pressure or pulse rate measures, weather through air pressure or temperature, and more in the future. Also, interesting possibilities exist in aggregating data from such sensors across devices to create data maps, but this is likely beyond the scope of most organizations for the short-term at least.

Apps

Input, output, sensing, and connecting are coordinated via software running on the underlying platform via application programming interfaces (APIs). APIs are interfaces to various features of the operating system, including available hardware. Different platforms have different operating systems and consequently software, but they share some characteristics. All the platforms have applications and connect to and through various networks.

Applications are needed to run on the mobile processor and to support various tasks. Some are built in and are viewed as meeting core needs. Increasingly, *app stores*, online markets that allow purchasing and downloading applications from a variety of developers, have created a broad variety of personalization and customization. The user or the organization can augment chosen capabilities by purchasing additional software from a suite of developed software. Users might choose tools to access information in a variety of ways or perform custom tasks. It is also getting easier for a reasonably skilled web designer to create applications.

Personal information management (PIM) involves the suite of core applications that characterized most early PDAs: notes or memos; contacts or addresses; calendar or events; and tasks or to-do lists. These personal productivity tools support user goals. Calculators are another classic addition, as are alarms.

Media viewers are core to certain devices, such as media players, but are appearing more generally. This starts with audio and video playback but includes viewing documents in a few or a variety of common document formats.

Media capture is also useful, whether for audio or video recording or text input. It's now possible to draw graphics on devices as well.

Web browsing is an increasingly frequent capability. I remember hearing several years ago that 75% of cell phones had a browser, and 75% of people did not know it. It is likely that it is essentially impossible to buy a phone without a browser, but users may not have data plans.

Communication is another common capability that applications provide. While phones provide voice and text messaging (simple messaging system, or SMS), more general devices can often accommodate e-mail and newer forms like instant messaging (IM) in a variety of formats from AOL, MSN, Yahoo, and Skype. Connections to social networking sites are also increasingly being enabled, such as Facebook and LinkedIn. Twitter, which crosses the categories of IM and social networking, is also increasingly represented. A new development is the ability to video chat, using additional cameras on the same side as the screen to support video conferencing. Apple's FaceTime is one new standard, and Skype supposedly is supporting this capability as well.

Custom applications are the new opportunity. As developers identify niches and create applications, such as taking advantage of sensors to create new forms of augmentation, it is possible to customize your quiver of tools. For instance, organizations can create their own unique applications as well as custom content, such as tapping into proprietary databases to match up unique information with publicly available information to provide new services.

Networking

Although synching with a desktop was a critical step for mobile devices to really succeed, thus creating a unified information environment, the original mechanism was through a physical cable, so updates were possible only when the device was next to the computer. However, networking technologies have broadened the reach and have started allowing much more complex and useful connections between the mobile device and the world. With the availability of the Internet and the ability to pair almost any piece of hardware with a mobile device, the opportunities become quite heady.

One new development is storing information not locally on the device or synching it to a personal computer but instead to servers hosted on the Internet, also known as *the cloud*. Increasingly, applications are being developed that are coupled to internet-based storage. The advantage here is that you can access the same information from any device, anywhere, rather than only synched devices, and don't have to worry about having sufficient storage. There are risks, however, in that any problems with the data provider could mean a loss of data, and privacy becomes an issue. Still, many are choosing to keep all their data in the cloud.

A variety of hardware devices exist to bring data from one machine to another. Universal serial bus (USB) devices can hold data and transfer between machines with an appropriate port. A variety of other formats similarly exist to carry data from one device to another (e.g., SD and MicroSD cards). Increasingly, however, there is strong interest in linking machines without physical connections.

Wireless networking technologies range from short distance (1–2 meters), sometimes known as *personal area networks* (PAN), through medium-area networks (100–200 meters), known as *local area networks* (LAN), to *wide area networks* (WAN), which are essentially ubiquitous. Different networking standards are involved.

Personal area networks typically use *Bluetooth*, a network standard that allows two devices to communicate. This can be a mobile device with a laptop or with peripherals (hands-free headsets, for example). This can also support other devices like keyboards and potentially other forms of input, output, and sensors.

New local area networking standards continue to emerge. For example, *near-field communication* is beginning to be common in supporting mCommerce (using mobile phones to conduct financial transactions).

Infrared is another technology that has been applied to certain uses. Using a low-level light source, infrared is a directional standard that offers relatively high bandwidth but only over short distances, and the two communicating devices must share a line of sight. For communication, the IrDA (Infrared Data Association) sets standards.

Local area networks are converging on wi-fi technologies. The 802.11x standard (where x currently can be b, g, or n, which are protocols for different speeds of transmission) provides a way for an internet access point to be shared among any devices having the capability. With wi-fi, mobile devices can access other local devices as if they were sharing a wired internet connection.

While new technologies are coming, the most prevalent way to get data to mobile devices without a wi-fi connection is through phone services. There are two major competing standards: *Code division multiple access (CDMA)* is less prevalent and is used in only a few countries; global system for mobile (GSM) is the standard in Europe and much of the rest of the world. While it is not necessary to know much more than this, it should be noted that the United States and several other countries use both largely incompatible systems, which serves as a barrier to enjoying the freedom and advances seen in other parts of the world, notably Europe and Japan. Both can provide, via subspecifications, various levels of data access as well as voice and text messaging (SMS and multimedia messaging systems, or MMSs). Subscriber identify module (SIM) cards are purchased and put into an appropriate phone to provide accounts for using the technologies.

As mentioned above, it is also possible to use voice without the use of the phone services, as VoIP provides a mechanism for delivering audio across the internet as a second channel.

New standards are emerging that may provide direct internet connections at distances similar to those achieved with cellular technologies. Just as with the hardware, networking is a dynamic area with ongoing efforts to provide improved access speeds.

OF PLATFORMS AND PROCESSING POWER

One issue that has dogged the mobile market is Adobe's Flash technology. Flash has been the *lingua franca* for web delivery of interactions based on rich graphics and flexibility of input, as it is available on pretty much every browser. As a consequence, most of the e-learning development tools have had Flash as their output format.

The problem, however, has been the performance of Flash on the weaker processors available in mobile devices. Battery power is the big issue, and the trade-off of performance for battery life has been generally accepted. As a result, most mobile devices have not supported Flash, so much e-learning content hasn't automatically been available for mobile delivery.

Several factors are changing this. For one, a richer web standard called HTML 5 is supposed to host the capabilities of Flash, and it may well be that when this standard is finalized it may have lower power requirements than Flash. As such, many tools are already or soon will be exporting HTML 5. At the same time, mobile processors are getting more powerful, and new devices are claiming that they can support Flash.

At this point, it is not clear what will finally occur first: whether HTML 5 will emerge as a solution or Flash will get more optimized and processors will finally be able to run it. The short-term result, however, is that the mechanism to deliver rich interactions is still largely in the hands of custom development rather than in a single cross-platform format.

FOUR C'S AND THINKING DIFFERENTLY

In my previous book on mobile learning, I characterized what I called the four C's of mobile capabilities: content, compute, capture, and communicate (Quinn, 2011). These provide one of several useful ways to think about mobile learning.

Content deals with the ability to store, or access, content on a device. The word here really means media: documents (text or graphics); audio; and video. Much can be accomplished by making content available to individuals when or where they are. We frequently see audio files or video files of lectures, interviews, and documentaries as well as documents of a variety of types, including textbooks, chapters, and articles.

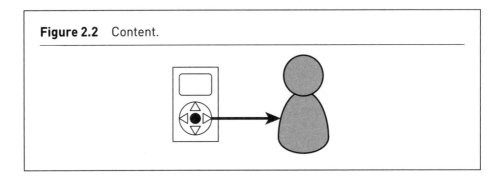

Figure 2.2 Content.

On the other hand, *capture* has to do with the individual producing content rather than accessing it. Individuals can capture pictures, audio, even video and can create images and text. Increasingly, devices can also record location as well. This data can be saved or shared. So people capture images of contexts and videos of performances and take notes while in the field.

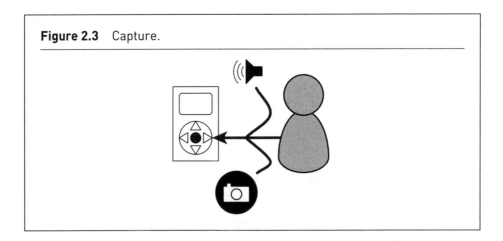

Figure 2.3 Capture.

One of the advantages these devices also provide, whether through built-in tools like calculators or through purchased or custom apps, is the ability to *compute* outcomes that humans have neither the working memory nor knowledge to calculate. So a learner could enter some observed parameters such as a quantity and area and calculate a density or something more complicated.

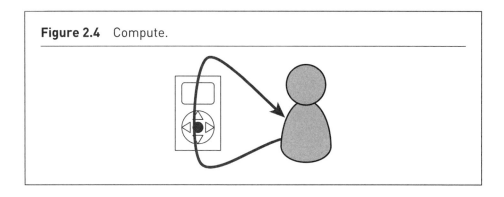

Figure 2.4 Compute.

When we share data, we *communicate*. Our devices let us fulfill our natural tendency to communicate, and they support synchronous or asynchronous interaction. We're moving from voice and text to live video chat and sharing the photos and videos we capture. Communications can occur with fellow learners, instructors, teaching or research assistants, experts, or anyone else within or external to the institution.

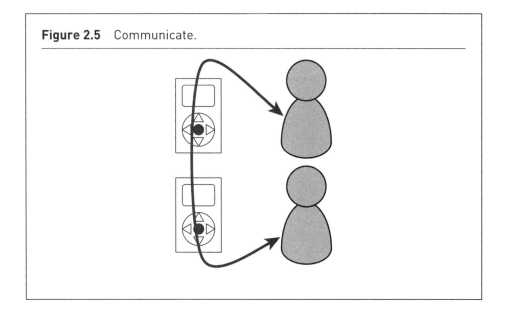

Figure 2.5 Communicate.

Combinations of the four C's are possible as well, such as communicating a captured image for collaborative support or capturing location as a basis for customizing content to be available. In all cases, these devices *augment* our cognitive capabilities. They provide the capabilities that our brains do not do well and vice versa. Together with these devices, we are a more powerful problem solver than without their portable capabilities.

Context

These capabilities are now available wherever we need them and are no different from what we achieve with desktops, with one caveat: Mobile devices have the unique property of being aware of the local context, via, for example, capture of GPS and local signals, and of doing things specific to that context. This, however, is an important distinction, and the opportunities are only recently beginning to be exploited.

Context sensitivity is an important opportunity. Our learners are mobile, and mobility takes them into different places. If those places are relevant to their learning experience, it has been up to their recollection, unless it has been an organized excursion. However, serendipity has been missed. Now, opportunistic conjunctions of location and learning goals can be capitalized on. So, for example, an architecture student might be able to tap into the history of a particular building, a history student could read about the events surrounding a location, or an engineering student could access the force equations associated with a structure.

One type of context that has been largely ignored so far is that of *when*, not where. We can know what people are doing, regardless of where they are, by their calendar (or, more granularly, what application they are using). We could provide context-specific information appropriate to the task, not the location. We do this to some extent based on the application, as it's built in, but we could also provide support before, during, and after an event to improve performance and scaffold learning.

DEFINITION

Having looked at mobile devices, what is mobile learning? Let us start with the definition the eLearning Guild used in its 2007 360° Mobile Learning Research Report (Wexler et al., 2007):

> Any activity that allows individuals to be more productive when consuming, interacting with, or creating information, mediated through a compact digital portable device that the individual carries on a regular basis, has reliable connectivity, and fits in a pocket or purse.

It is important to note that the focus is on being more productive. When people hear the term *mobile learning*, the initial reaction tends to be about courses on the phone. Yet most mobile learning applications really are not about full courses but instead are more about performance support, helping individuals in the moment. The nature of mobile is its relatively short, though perhaps many, uses a day. This maps better to support information needs in context rather than addressing a major skill gap with a full learning design.

Think about how you use your cell phone, PDA, or whatever mobile device you use regularly. Do you tend to spend a long time with it, or do you use it to quickly capture or access information? The usual pattern, as documented by Palm (2003), is that desktop computers get used only a few times per day but for long periods of different use. On the other hand, mobile devices tend to get used many times a day for quick access: to make a call, to capture an event or a note, to look up some information.

The quick access that characterizes mobile use is very much about support in the moment rather than a formal learning experience. In either case, however, there are some commonalities in underlying ways to look at interactions with mobile devices.

SUMMARY

This chapter presents reasons mobile devices make us smarter in the moment and will provide some of the benefits to the higher education experience. These same capabilities also can provide the opportunity to make us smarter over time, which is where we get into learning.

PRACTICE

1. How do or could you access content on a mobile device to make you smarter?

2. How do or could you capture information (e.g., photo, video, audio, notes) to augment your ability to perform?

3. What computational apps or support do you use?

4. How are you, or could you be, accessing others to make yourself more efficient or effective?

Foundations: Learning

To take advantage of mLearning capabilities, we have to understand learning if we wish to fully capitalize on the potential. This may seem a bit redundant or even presumptuous given the audience, but it is important if nothing else to have a shared vocabulary. Also, we should recognize that what has been the status quo in the classroom was designed for industrial age efficiency rather than natural effectiveness, so we briefly review learning with a focus on formal change. Note that much of what we see in classrooms doesn't follow even the good principles of learning *in* classrooms.

We start with the way we naturally learn. How do we learn before schooling? There we find the seven C's of learning (Quinn, 2009c), to complement the four C's of mobile learning (Quinn, 2011):

- We *choose* what is important to us.
- We *commit* to it, with persistence.
- We *create*, whether product or performance.
- Occasionally we *crash*.
- We *converse* with others to understand.
- We *copy*, as we look at other's work and performance and model ours on it.
- We *collaborate*, working with others.

Interestingly, failure is an important part of learning, and the social learning is not just to be accepted but also encouraged: Copying isn't bad, talking together isn't wrong, and collaborating is to be desired. While this is an informal characterization, it is very much a social constructivist viewpoint, an integration of theorists as varied as Bruner (1961) and Vygotsky (1978), as well as many others.

This suggests that when we want to design learning we need to help learners understand why it's important so they choose to participate and to set expectations appropriately so that they are willing to commit. Learners should be actively creating. And we should ensure that they receive feedback about their success and failure, are appropriately resourced with support to ultimately succeed, and ideally can share tasks and learning with one another.

Our approach to creating learning traditionally has manifested in a design process that can be relatively generically characterized as:

- Identifying the learning objective and the audience
- Characterizing the desired performance and developing the final assessment
- Developing a learning experience that is aligned to success on that assessment
- Evaluating and refining to achieve the objective

This process can be followed using most design approaches such as Dick, Carey, and Carey's (2004) systematic design of instruction, the ADDIE model of Analysis, Design, Development, Implementation, and Evaluation, and so on. What results can then roughly be categorized in a similarly generic way as learning elements of:

- An introduction that helps learners understand:
  - Why this is important emotionally and societally
  - What they'll be doing and able to do
  - Relevant knowledge
- A concept presentation of the model that guides performance
- Examples that demonstrate how that concept is applied in a context:
  - With explication of underlying thinking that guides the performance
  - That ideally demonstrates backtracking and repair

- Practice opportunities in applying the concept to contexts:
  - With examples and practice contexts together spanning the space of appropriate transfer
  - With alternatives that address reliable misconceptions that learners demonstrate, and individualized feedback
  - With feedback that relates their performance to the concept
  - Starting with tasks within the learners' grasp and gradually progressing to the full performance
- A summary that closes the experience:
  - Cognitively by indicating:
    - What they are now capable of
    - What they are subsequently ready to explore
    - Where they might find more information
  - Emotionally celebrating their effort and ultimate success

This is an admittedly idiosyncratic collection centered on the cognitive apprenticeship framework of Collins, Brown, and Holum (1991) and is informed by elements of Reigeluth and Stein's (1983) elaboration theory; Keller's (1983) ARCS (attention, relevance, confidence, satisfaction) model; Spiro, Feltovich, Jacobsen, and Coulson's (1989) cognitive flexibility theory; and Van Merriënboer's (1997) four component instructional design. It is also an editorial stance. The emphasis is on cognitive skills rather than on attitudinal shift or motor performance. It may seem contrary to the previously suggested constructivist approach, but the order is traditional; other pedagogies may reorder the elements, so a problem-based learning approach à la Barrows (1986) might put the practice first. It is also for designed instruction, so there does have to be a recognition that the environment and resources need to be planned to succeed. Learning design is, ultimately, a probabilistic endeavor. Our goal is to increase the likelihood that the desired performance is achieved, and the proposed elements are an integrated attempt to do just that.

While you may quibble with bits and pieces of what is presented here, it serves as a framework to think about how we apply mobile technologies to achieve learning. One point is to recognize that, by being clearly discrete about the learning functions that different content development efforts serve, we can decouple them from a learning event and start thinking about how we might use them discretely to serve a more distributed learning model.

MAKING LEARNING WORK

From a cognitive perspective, our learning goals are twofold: We want *retention* of the knowledge or skill over time until needed; and we want to *transfer* that capability to all appropriate problems (and no inappropriate ones). There are things that facilitate each goal and also some common practices that minimize the likelihood of those occurring.

Objectives

Good learning starts with good objectives, from which you can align the practice tasks (the assignments) and then the concepts and examples to support success. One of the major failures in most formal education, in my experience, is having objectives that are pure knowledge and not applied. This may seem like a strong statement, but personal experience over decades in higher education teaching and publishing both from personal involvement and from a business standpoint has not convinced me otherwise.

There is a distinction between knowledge and application of that knowledge. As Alfred North Whitehead (1929) said, "Theoretical ideas should always find important applications within the pupil's curriculum . . . . The problem of keeping knowledge alive, of preventing it from becoming inert, which is the central problem of all education" (p. 5).

Cognitive science talks about *inert knowledge*, which can be recited on a test but will not get activated into conscious awareness where it is specifically relevant in practice. Actually applying knowledge—specifically how the learner should be applying it to solve problems—is important both to support learning and to ensure utility. In fact, if there is no application of the knowledge, the value of the content should be questioned. Ideally, learners would not just understand concepts but also would use them to make predictions, explanations, and decisions.

In the most extreme case, you would only focus on application objectives without worrying about taxonomies or levels of specification. Brenda Sugrue

(2002) rightly pointed out the problems with Bloom's taxonomy (Bloom, 1956) and the alternatives, including this extreme position of assuming application-oriented objectives. However, cognitive science and educational psychology at least offer better choices that are more aligned with how individuals solve problems in the world, providing a better basis on which to choose objectives.

Perhaps surprisingly for a cognitive scientist, I have a great appreciation for Mager's (1975) format for objectives, stipulating that a good objective has at least three things: (1) a statement of the conditions or context of performance; (2) a statement of the task; and (3) a measurable way to evaluate that performance.

Now, this is a push not for a vocational shift in education but instead for support for the effectiveness of the learning. Even at the far edge of the training–education continuum, where the learning goals are characterized by transfer of the knowledge (i.e., broad principles rather than specific training), the focus needs to be on ensuring that knowledge is available for use. If a curriculum is not to be used, why is it being covered?

To put it another way, I am strongly advocating focusing on competency-based, not normative, performance. Define what successful performance is and allow all learners to achieve it if they are capable; don't grade on a curve. And those competencies should be closely coupled to real performance that makes a difference in the world.

It can be hard to get subject matter experts (SMEs) to talk about the skills as opposed to knowledge. As part of our cognitive architecture, our expertise becomes unavailable for conscious inspection, and we have to rely on introspection. Consistently, this introspection proves to be unreliable. One of the consequences is that experts revert to the knowledge they learned. The requirement is for more work on the part of the instructor or learning designer to consciously reframe the focus. A useful heuristic, based on a variety of influences, is to focus on the decisions that learners will be able to make that they cannot make now.

Practice

In a linear order, the learner's experience would start with an introduction, which suggests that this would be the first element you design. However, in a focused design process, you need to define the assessment after you specify the objective, because you want the actual task the learner performs to be tightly coupled to the learning objective. This increases the likelihood that the overall learning is aligned to achieve the desired outcome. The term *practice* is used to keep the focus on the learner developing practical and applied skills, the real key to achieving meaningful outcomes.

In *Engaging Learning: Designing e-Learning Simulation Games* (Quinn, 2005), I wrote about the principles of aligning engaging experiences with effective practice. Next to mentored real practice, simulation games are the best form of practice (and mentored real practice doesn't scale well: mentors are finite resources, and in real practice mistakes can be costly). The alignment highlighted the following elements:

- *Clear (or emergent) goal*: the ultimate desired outcome of the activity should be(come) apparent.

- *Appropriate challenge*: the task should be hard enough to avoid boredom but not so challenging as to be frustrating.

- *An integrating story*: the action should be set in a thematically coherent world.

- *Meaningful link between action and story:* what the learner does impacts the storyline.

- *Meaningful link between learner and story*: the learner has to care about the problem embodied in the world.

- *Active exploration*: the learner must make choices and discover the consequences, not just see the question and then the answer.

- *Direct manipulation*: the learner must act on the represented world of the problem in a method as close to the real mechanism as possible.

- *Appropriate feedback*: the consequences of choices should be conveyed in ways that reflect how the world would react (and ultimately should communicate via the concept of why the choice was right or wrong).

- *Novelty*: ideally, there is unpredictability in the outcome, or at least some unexpected components rather than linear and deterministic outcomes.

While this framework constitutes an ideal, one of its important outcomes is that you can create better learning practice with familiar elements. While the ultimate embodiment is a simulation-governed interaction, even branching scenarios or better written multiple-choice questions can embody these principles. The goal is to create a setting where learners have to make a decision that applies the concepts they are learning in ways that solve contextualized problems and in ways that mimic how that knowledge gets applied in the world outside of the classroom.

A few heuristics help. As mentioned earlier, focusing on decisions helps maintain a focus on meaningful application. A second trick is to elicit the ways learners reliably go wrong. These *reliable misconceptions* provide opportunities to address the ways learners bring in inappropriate information, as VanLehn's (1990) research suggested. The alternatives to the right answer, whether in multiple-choice questions or game decisions, are the ways learners continue to err. This helps frame the desired challenge, which is particularly important in formative practice, before it counts.

The SMEs who can be problematic when trying to extract the application, not just the knowledge, are actually a great boon in another way. One of the tricks to finding out the ways to frame the problem is to understand why the experts find this particular domain of practice interesting. There is a reason they have chosen this field, and if you can tap into that passion, you have a hook on which to catch the learner's interest. This helps frame both forms of meaningfulness of the task.

Two associated and important concepts are the spacing of practice and the scaffolding. For the former, while the parameters differ depending on how often you will apply the information and how complex it is, overall we know that *massed practice*, that is, a bunch of practice right before a test, leads to little retention over time. Retention drops off quickly unless practice is appropriately spaced (Thalheimer, 2006). On the other hand, if learning is spaced and then practiced, retention can be quite persistent (see Figure 3.1). Consequently, considering the right suite of practice problems, raising the level of challenge, and spacing out over time constitute several of the important components of learning design (and a mobile opportunity).

For the latter concept, it is important that the practice problems range in difficulty from what learners can initially do until the final practice challenges have the level of complexity sufficient to lead to successful performance outside the learning experience. Consequently, initial and intermediate practice will have *scaffolding*: qualitative or quantitatively simple computations, having parts of the problems already completed, or certain complications avoided initially. The goal is to have the challenge level maintained relative to the learner's increasing competence.

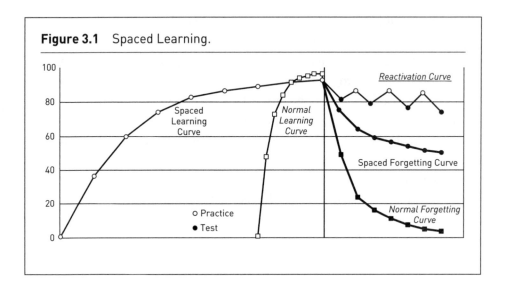

Figure 3.1 Spaced Learning.

One outcome of learner activity is the creation of products that represent learner understanding. This includes text documents but can also be represented in media files, whether audio or video. The ability to create media is typically viewed as an important component of so-called 21st-century skills.

Requiring or allowing a variety of media supports the development of communication as a separate skill on top of the domain and is a powerful tool for learners to share not only their capabilities but also their understandings. A *director's notes* version of a video of a performance, where the learner includes the thoughts behind the representation, is a very useful way to investigate what they are thinking.

Concepts

Once we have decided objectives and meaningful practice, we should have a good idea of what concepts provide the guidance for performance. The term *concepts* here means interrelated principles that form models or frameworks that are applied in particular contexts. For example, the *law of supply and demand*, *photosynthesis*, and *metaphor* are all concepts that play a role in various domains. It turns out that our brains are not suitably structured for remembering rote knowledge and procedures but work well with frameworks and models. We can regenerate missing steps from such concepts, but if we are recalling rote steps and forget one we have little basis for repair.

Research on mental models has shown that we are good working with presented models but have trouble abstracting appropriate models from examples, as Gick and Holyoak's (1980, 1983) work on analogical reasoning suggested. Similarly, in general we work better with qualitative model reasoning before we deal with the associated quantitative problem solving. Typically, we build models if we are not presented with them, and if those models we build are wrong we don't replace them upon contrary evidence but instead *patch* them, which leads to inefficient application.

On the other hand, models are powerful bases for reasoning. By *running* the models, we can predict consequences and explain outcomes. Thus, we also have a basis for decision making, the ultimate outcome. Individuals equipped with models are more resilient in the face of adversity than those with rote procedures.

To convey models, conceptual representations are helpful. Text is a powerful communicator, but our cognitive architecture also supports using visual representations. Diagrams and animations (for dynamic situations) are valuable media. Further, Spiro et al.'s (1992) cognitive flexibility theory suggests that multiple representations facilitate comprehension and application. I propose that multiple representations increase the likelihood that a learner will find one that resonates and then will support the acquisition of the rest. Further, multiple representations also increase the likelihood that, in a problem-solving situation, a representation will be activated and then can increase the number of available relevant models that can be applied, thus increasing the likelihood of reaching a solution. And given that learning and problem solving are a probabilistic game, such improvements are to be desired.

As a consequence, finding multiple ways to communicate the concept is valuable. Larkin and Simon (1987) documented the value of mapping the conceptual relationships from a model to the spatial relationships of a diagram. Thus, if you have an appropriate concept, you should always *at least* be able to complement a text recitation of the concept with a diagram or animation.

Examples

Coupled with the content are the examples, which demonstrate how the concepts are applied in context. Two important components of examples that really work are exposing the underlying thought processes that accompany application and the breadth of context.

As mentioned already, SMEs have trouble articulating what they actually do, yet Alan Shoenfeld's (1992) work on mathematics examples suggests that having access to the underlying thoughts that map the concepts to the particular features of the context is important for learners. Whether the media for such annotation are labels on steps in documents, voice-overs on audio or video stories, or thought bubbles on comic strips or graphic novels, the alternatives considered and how the concept guides the performance are important to convey.

An additional benefit is to demonstrate mistakes and repairs. It is hard for experts to perform mistakes, particularly in public, but in reality experts often make mistakes. There are two benefits to helping learners realize this and modeling the self-monitoring and repair process: helping prevent damage to learner self-esteem when mistakes are made; and helping learners internalize that self-improvement process.

One important aspect of using examples is ensuring the coverage of contexts. Learners abstract the space of application of a concept from the contexts seen across examples and practice. It is important to ensure that the examples seen use contexts that complement the contexts seen in practice and together provide a representative coverage of the relevant space of use of the concept.

The stories and contexts chosen for the examples, within the constraint of using sufficient breadth, should also be as compelling and relevant for the learner as possible, as Bransford et al.'s anchored instruction (Cognition and Technology Group at Vanderbilt, 1990) supports. The same principles of meaningfulness seen for practice contexts should be also seen in examples to address the affective or emotional (really, *conative*) side of learning as well as the cognitive.

Summaries

The learning experience typically concludes, appropriately, with a recitation of what learners have accomplished, what they are now able to do, and what further directions they can pursue. However, one more thing can and should be addressed: the associated emotional experience.

Learners have invested effort and endured challenge (and potentially some frustration and boredom). Ideally, you would recognize each learner's individual experience, but at least acknowledge the overall experience.

Introductions

There are emotional components to be addressed not only in the summary (and in the meaningfulness components in practice and examples) but also in the introduction.

The very first things learners should experience is a visceral exposure to why this content is important. Ausubel's (1978) work demonstrated that learning is facilitated by activating relevant prior knowledge (and this should be part of the introduction), but I suggest that opening up learners emotionally to the importance of the coming experience is also part of optimizing the learning.

In addition to the reference examples that are used to illustrate application of concept to context, it is helpful to use examples that motivate the forthcoming learning and elicit a wry recognition that understanding this concept *is* appropriate for the learner. You can choose to be humorous or dramatic or to exaggerate the positive or negative consequences of this knowledge, but you really should open up the learner's motivation.

Another component to successfully dealing with the *emotional* side of the learning experience is to appropriately set expectations. A mismatch between the learner's expectations and the experience can produce dissatisfaction and impede learning. Consequently, setting expectations about, for example, what will likely be hard, what will be easy, and what might be kind of dry is a worthwhile investment.

Finally, a proper introduction helps contextualize the importance of the learning content in terms of the broader picture of what is happening in the world. This can be coincident with setting the visceral understanding of the importance, but it may also not be the case. If not, then a separate transition from the world to the specific learning is a valuable exercise.

BEYOND THE BASICS

We can extend beyond individual formal linear learning in a number of ways. There are alternate pedagogies, for one. We also need to look at the social aspects of learning, as some will argue that not all learning is social. We should also look at learning to learn, which, in this era of decreasing half-life of information, may need to be the main role for formal education. And we should not ignore considering performance support and what needs to be learned versus what should be looked up or computed. Finally, we should look at what is on the horizon.

Alternate Pedagogies

While the traditional order of presentation is introduction > concept > example > practice > summary, other orders are possible. Figure 3.2 shows common approaches including problem based, navigable, and adaptive.

In Barrows's (1986) problem-based learning, an overarching practice task is presented first, and the rest of the elements are arranged around the task. In this situation, the problem provides much of the motivation that the introduction normally serves and drives interest in the associated concept, examples, and relevant practices that will lead to the ability to ultimately complete the practice.

Rather than pre-script the approach, an alternative in asynchronous and independent learning is to make the content navigable so that learners can choose what aspect they wish to accomplish. While progression may be blocked to

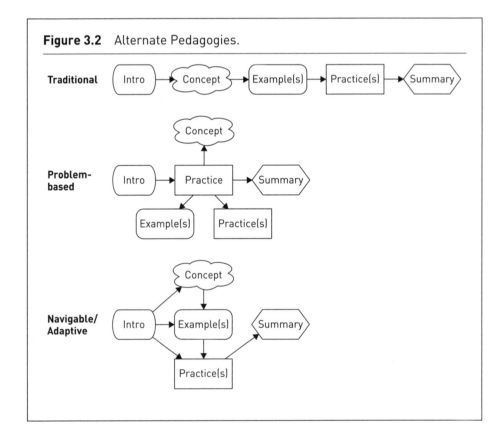

Figure 3.2 Alternate Pedagogies.

further learning units until completion is signaled by successful execution of whatever final practice is deemed the necessary evaluation, learners are free to choose to explore concepts and examples and to attempt practices under their own initiative. A default sequence may be provided for those with less confidence or capability in self-directed learning.

An alternative is to deliver an adaptive experience, which recommends examples, concepts, or more based on a variety of factors including knowledge of the domain, learner preferences, or even learner characteristics. Such capabilities are possible, though the research basis for adapting learning is still under development.

Social Learning

As was suggested initially but has not been addressed to this point is that learning is not (and indeed some argue *cannot* be) individual but instead is social. Learner–mentor interactions are one thing, but learner–learner interactions also have valuable outcomes. As mentioned already, a variety of influences are at work here.

The primary argument I suggest is that social interaction leads to tighter cycles of content engagement: Negotiation of shared understanding requires revisiting the content topic under alternate possibilities to converge upon an interpretation. This can occur just by hearing other viewpoints but also can be assigned to teams to determine a joint response to an issue, or even more rigorously, producing a shared solution to a problem. Designing social interactions requires greater consideration of the ability for learners to coordinate activities, but the learning outcomes can be more beneficial.

The ability to see other performances and to internalize not only the performances but also their monitoring (i.e., the cognitive strategies regulating behavior) is a second important opportunity. In this sense, copying isn't necessarily bad.

As a side note, the most valuable role of the instructor in an ideal learning situation is not to present content but to design activity and facilitate reflection (Laurillard, 1993). Although instructors can present valuable information, this should not be to the exclusion of assessing individual comprehension and guiding acquisition of the requisite thinking skills.

Learning to Learn

A final consideration for learning is the learner's *meta-learning,* or learning to learn skills. Taking these for granted, particularly in higher education, may seem appropriate, but the evidence is that such an assumption is not warranted. There is an opportunity to develop such skills as a conscious component of the learning experience.

Much is made both principally and pragmatically of the 21st-century skills: the necessary learning, thinking, and problem-solving skills in the information era. These typically are dealt with not on an individual basis but within the context of meaningful activity in a domain. Consequently, they serve as a layer on top of regular activity.

Another way to think about learning to learn is how to learn via mobile. Are there new mobile literacies? Parry (2011) thinks that there are. He suggests that the quickness of access is new, that there are times when multitasking makes sense (and conversely), and that understanding the vast data being collected is important. The latter underpins some of the new opportunities afforded by the topics we explore in Chapter Eight. Information literacy certainly will be important as well as understanding the ramifications of mobile data and information usage, whether for good or ill.

Performance Support

While performance support is typically considered an alternative to formal learning, it can also be considered an adjunct. The scaffolding around practice can be delivered by job aids and tools as well as by simplified problems. Similarly, the original intent of Gery's (1995) electronic performance support systems was not just to streamline performance but also to develop the performer's individual ability as well. While these systems are seldom seen in practice, their promise is real, and they present an opportunity to be taken advantage of.

While most of the higher education opportunities for performance support will fall within organizational needs, considering the ways that learner performance can be supported should not be ignored. A major university's veterinary program developed a tool for learners that was so successful, graduates asked if they could have their own copies in their practice. Imagine the benefits of having such a tool to disseminate to alumni.

Rossett (e.g., Rossett & Shafer, 2006) categorizes support as planners, which offer support pre- or post-event, sidekicks, and which support performance in the moment. Documents can support both of these needs well. Documents can also maintain more traditional content roles in formal learning, and video and audio can provide some performance support but are more typically used for formal presentation. Performance support can also come in the form of compute, where calculations that are helpful in the moment but that are beyond the learner's capabilities without digital support are also useful. Graphing calculators, for instance, remain a common and useful mobile support device, though these capabilities are now being supported on more generic mobile devices as well. We will start with performance support in the next chapter.

SUMMARY

To complement the previous chapter's background on mobile devices, we reviewed an enlightened view of learning. These are the two components necessary to take full advantage of mobile opportunities to augment the student experience. With this foundation in place, we can move on to consider how mobile can be used in different areas of the higher education institution function.

PRACTICE

1. How could mobile devices enhance introductions to the content?

2. How might you use mobile technologies to present concepts in different ways?

3. What ways could you use mobile devices to support communicating examples?

4. What are some opportunities that might be provided for mobile practice?

5. How are you incorporating 21st-century skills into your curriculum, and how can mobile help?

Administration "To Go"

Key point: Meet core needs simply.

In addition to the formal learning roles in which mobile technologies can play a part, there are administrative tasks related to learning that institutions must support and where mobile can also assist. In this chapter, we review those additional areas of support. We are concerned here with student-related tasks like registration and enrollment and information services that could be of interest to the student and aided by mobile. There are roles for mobile in nonlearner-focused organizational activities, but they are covered better in other places (e.g., Quinn, 2011). Here the focus is very definitely on performance support, not on formal learning.

The systematic way to examine opportunities to improve the student experience and outcomes is by using the broad picture, an *environmental scan* (Figure 4.1). By stepping back it is possible to see societal factors that surround institutional components, including the learning experience.

Beyond the interaction of learners with each other, with content, and with their mentor, there are the goals of the program as well as the culture and setting both programmatically and institutionally. The expectations of students and the pedagogical expectations of the program are important, as is the physical plant that will dictate how much blended learning, or distribution of learning experience across channels (e.g., face to face, online, mobile), is possible and necessary.

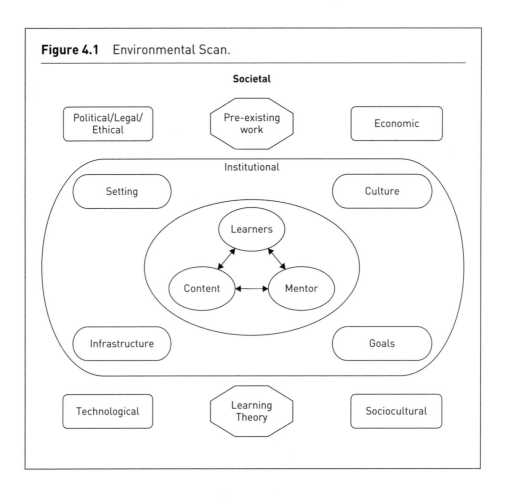

Figure 4.1 Environmental Scan.

More broadly, there are likely economic pressures on the ability to do technology development and learner preparation. Legal issues like equity of access will play a factor in what you can or cannot propose. Accreditation may provide barriers to the use of mobile technologies as well. Each of these considerations may offer opportunities as well as constraints on what makes sense for your situation.

Within the infrastructure, there a variety of specific higher education structures, processes, and goals. Many of these such as campus maintenance and human resources are incidental to student learning and have indirect relationships to the actual teaching but not direct connections. You also see many roles, again some directly relevant, and some incidental. Faculty, and learning design staff in particular, play key roles. For our purposes here, we want to look at student-facing functions and personnel, leaving the primary-learning, classroom-aligned tasks for subsequent chapters.

PRINCIPLES

The perspective we should take is very much a combination of performance support and interaction design. An overall principle is that whatever you can enable through technology, you might also want to make available via mobile. Increasingly, students may eschew not just the computer lab but their laptop, preferring instead a tablet or a mobile phone. Oklahoma University, for instance, conducted an experiment with iPads that returned positive reviews (CNET, 2011). In that context, ensuring mobile access makes sense.

A second perspective may also be relevant. Using technology may be a factor in efficiencies. If learners can accommodate more desires using self-help via technology, resources may be reorganized for more effective use.

Two major perspectives exist: (1) to make mobile-accessible features that are already delivered via technology, such as whatever is already available through the university web site (leaving the decision to expand other access to the broader technology perspective while suggesting that mobile now be considered automatically as well); and (2) to capitalize on mobile capabilities to consider new opportunities.

The first step is to consider how mobile accessible the institution site is. Is the institution site usable via mobile access? Are the associated services, including any learning tools, able to be used via the mobile web? In addition to the important information architecture issues related to ensuring that the site meets the needs of the visitors, the question is whether the site is usable when accessed by mobile web browsers. This is an important first step to meeting campus needs.

The main approach to a mobile-accessible site is to automatically generate one via using web standards, programmatically removing images, and streamlining text. The top-level domain for the mobile (.mobi) domain maintains a resource site that supports optimizing and testing your site for mobile accessibility (mtld.mobi, 2011). Many universities now provide mobile-accessible versions of their sites; examples are Virginia Tech (mobile.vt.edu), Massachusetts Institute of Technology (MIT; m.mit.edu), and Ohio State (m.osu.edu).

Beyond the traditional university site, specific mobile needs might well be met by specific application development. Major student-focused administration roles are admissions and enrollment, financial aid, research, student activities oversight such as clubs and sports, counseling and health services, library access, safety, and campus computing. These all have student interactions that can be beneficially enabled through technology.

Students have a variety of needs, ranging from primary needs like food and shelter to navigating and communicating to the full suite of administrative services. From a student perspective, administrative interactions center on:

- Registering
- Adding and dropping classes
- Getting grades
- Getting transcripts
- Searching for and renewing books in the library
- Reviewing administrative information such as financial aid eligibility
- Applying for financial support
- Requesting counseling or medical appointments
- Asking for computing help
- Information including navigation, weather, and perhaps shopping

An additional service that has become tragically important is emergency notification, which involves sending announcements via simple messaging system (SMS) to deal with catastrophic events, whether natural or man-made.

The principles are simple: What needs do students have for information and transactions on campus? What trips do they make to various offices, and could they accomplish those goals online and on the go? Can they make appointments? Can they search before they trek? What information might they want about how to get to campus, where to go near campus, and how to get there? What information do they need about the campus itself?

The C's

Included in the four C's are *content*, where you can provide learners with campus maps and transportation timetables; *compute*, where you can provide learners with tools (like choosing appointment times); *capture*, where you can survey them about campuswide issues or collect their photos and videos of campus events; and *communicate*, which involves providing contacts with faculty members, offices, and other students (within privacy constraints).

For content, the approach is to think through what information would be of use to the learner. Students may need to get to campus and get around on it, so maps of transit routes and the campus as well as schedules of the various forms of public transit could be made available. Bike and parking rules might also make sense. Students, whether resident or commuter, might want to know where on campus and nearby to purchase various commodities, such as pharmacy items, food (including menus), groceries, clothing, and gifts. Campus news and events could also be listed as well as hours of availability for various locations on campus, including dining locations, libraries, offices, and professors. Information could be provided on procedures for dealing with any administrative tasks, such as job aids for adding and dropping classes, making appointments, and searching the library applying for aid.

Using compute capabilities, we would want to enable some of the same tasks. We can allow students to arrange appointments, reserve tickets for music or sporting events, submit forms, and search the library. We could also calculate schedules from proposed class lists and support experimenting with different classes to see what the effects are on schedule, completion, and program options.

With capture capabilities, students could share pictures from events, reviews, or notes of events or facilities and could share other thoughts. If they're talking with a counselor, they could submit notes beforehand that help a counselor prepare for the session or provide updates on any ongoing issue. Another capture possibility is to collect information *from* students, such as survey data or other audience research.

Finally, via communicate capabilities, students can connect with each other around events or make arrangements to meet, send out invitations, find clubs, or organize their own, and more. While these capabilities can be arranged through existing tools, supporting the sharing of reviews of campus dining opportunities, sports events, and more can provide useful feedback both for potential users as well as for the institution itself.

Combining the initial four C's takes us further, allowing capture of location to show "you are here" on a map and to provide directions to a desired destination. Much of this is already available via existing mobile tools, but awareness may support the institution consciously augmenting information to provide richer capabilities. Could more information be provided to link Google capabilities to campus information services, for instance?

Channels

As a second approach, we can think through the channels we have at hand, such as documents, media (audio and video), voice, text messages, e-mail, and interactive, which can support multiple activities.

John Traxler, coeditor of *Mobile Learning: A Handbook for Educators and Trainers* (Kukulska-Hulme & Traxler, 2005) and professor of mobile learning at the University of Wolverhampton, told me how institutions are now recognizing that many devices are out there and that attention is shifting from the devices the university provides to the devices the students already have. At least in the United Kingdom, SMS had become a mainstream mechanism for university administration because it is equitable; pretty much everyone has a cell phone.

Text messages might be used not only for information distribution but also for interaction, as key words could be used to respond and provide more information and even to accomplish interactions.

Voice has potential as well. Reminders can certainly be sent out for due dates. Voice menus can be navigated to get specific information. A combination of voice and keypad presses could accomplish specific goals.

Mobile web certainly has the possibility of supporting both information and interaction. Web forms can be used to go beyond navigation to allow searches, reservations, and more. This is already being done in many instances through the web, but mobile access increases accessibility.

Finally, custom applications, including information delivery, interaction, and calculations, provide the opportunity to develop essentially any interaction desired. A custom suite of capabilities centered on the institution could provide not only services but also a branding opportunity. A community version that gives access to neighbors who use the university events would also be a potentially beneficial opportunity.

DELIVERY

There are both vendor-provided software and mobile solutions for these administrative needs, and other solutions are being developed. When a company like Google makes the announcement that it is now designing for mobile first and desktop second, a major shift has occurred (Google, 2010). Such thinking needs to penetrate the mind-set of administration services as well. This is a strong call to university information technology (IT) departments.

Infrastructure

In the learning management system (LMS) market, the commercial LMS solutions are Blackboard, Desire2Learn, and eCollege (now Pearson Learning Studio). The web site for Blackboard (2011), a major learning management system for higher education, cites that its mobile administration module supports a campus directory, campus maps, a course catalog, news, events, transit options, the library, and campus information such as images and videos and includes a mechanism to get help. Some of these may be occasional needs, and others can be very valuable in context. Desire2Learn, on the other hand, is currently limited to Blackberry platforms but similarly provides a rich suite of capabilities. Pearson's Learning Studio (the transition of eCollege) is using mobile web to deliver services around their learning requirements. Services such as deadlines and grade books are accessible to those institutions that enable such access.

The student information systems market is largely dominated by SunGard and PeopleSoft. SunGard (2010) also announced mobile interface to its suite of higher education software under the Banner label, which provides a rich suite of administrative capability. PeopleSoft's campus system is likely under development as well.

Applications

Going beyond what vendors are providing, the alternate approach is for the institution, or a consortium, to develop its own solutions. A number of institutions have taken this approach, using resources either from the computer science department or the core IT services to meet the need.

Abilene Christian University (2011) has been a leader in mobile applications and provides students with an iPod Touch (or iPhone, if the student arranges phone service). This has driven vibrant mobile development. Their vision of a suite of administrative capabilities includes emergency information, a financial services suite of purchasing and payments, campus information, and contact.

The Mobile Oxford (2011) project is a mobile web-based application developed with research funding that looks to provide a suite of useful capabilities. Included are a contact directory, library search, grades, news, weather, locations, status of computing services, news, and community information.

Stanford University (2011) too has developed a suite of mobile apps, including a tour, a link to lectures at iTunes University, and library search. They deliver both as mobile apps and via mobile web.

You could do more: a scavenger hunt or other game could allow visitors to familiarize themselves with the campus. Red 7 (2011), a web services company, built a text-messaging (SMS) game for outdoor art installations that serves as a model for such applications.

Design

Particularly for support applications rather than learning ones, certain perspectives are important. *The Path to Enlightenment* is a site documenting the mobile principles that guided the design of Palm applications (Palm, 2003). Indicated there are principles like understanding the nature of mobile use (quick access) rather than desktop use, focusing on the few features that will meet most of the need, involving users in design, and adding capabilities as the context changes.

As with all good design, the place to start is with usability and with thinking through the students' goals. What do they want and need to do? What can you do to help? User-centered design makes sense.

Some heuristics can aid in this process. What tasks do they need to do, and can you create a way to make it easier? And nothing's too trivial; one valuable application has been a mobile way to get updated on the status of dryers in the dorms at Stanford. It's about meeting needs and desires that exist or emerge.

Involve the intended audience in the design process. Have students suggest functions, review prototypes, even participate on the design team. As many computer and information systems programs start to offer courses on mobile solutions and development, it may make sense to consider involving instructors and students in mobile solutions development.

SUMMARY

Across these examples, some principles emerge. The emergent categories include location information such as navigation and weather, information such as events and news, social connections, and transactions such as office administration.

The options for delivery include mobile services through vendor capabilities, mobile web, and custom application. The former is easiest, but with trade-offs in flexibility and lock-in. The second approach is the most flexible. I recommend that apps be reserved for specific needs that are not needed by all or to meet needs that simply can't be met by mobile web, such as context-specific uses.

Do not assume that it has to be an app; a mobile web interface or SMS (as used in the United Kingdom) may be more successful. And your enterprise software may already have this capability. The important point is to develop the capabilities that students need.

PRACTICE

1. What administrative mobile capabilities does your LMS already provide (or the one you are or should be considering)?
2. How mobile accessible is the institution's web site?
3. What big impacts on the student experience could you make with mobile capabilities on your campus or for your institution?

TASK CHECKLIST

Enrollment
- Class availability list
- Class sign-up
- Class drop

Travel
- Campus map
- Transit options
- Nearby resources

Knowledge
- Event calendar
- News

- Weather
- Services status
- Campus cams
- Frequently asked questions
- Schedules and deadlines
- Directory

Community
- Clubs and societies
- Campus network (photos, videos, interests)

Services
- Library search and reserve
- Library assistance
- Health and safety information
- Health appointments
- Counseling information
- Academic counseling appointments
- Financial services
- Computing services assistance
- Emergency information sign-up and broadcasts

5

Content Is King

Key point: Smaller chunks, more frequently.

When we are moving from mobile opportunities in administration to learning, we need a structured way to proceed. For me, the right way is to look at the elements of learning: for example, introduction, concept, example, practice. From a cognitive perspective, the primary distinctions for individuals are content consumption versus interactive knowledge and skill application. Here, we focus on content, and in a subsequent chapter we'll deal with interaction before we go on to extend beyond the individual into social situations.

As indicated by the first C of the four C's of mobile capabilities, *content*, the ability to drive (or pull) content onto a mobile device is a major opportunity. Content can serve several instructional purposes, as discussed earlier. Introductions, concept presentations, examples, and summaries are all natural content areas. Content that is associated with practice activities, such as job aids and performance support, also qualify. Having covered the elements of learning earlier, here we look at the various media and the role they play.

MEDIA

Content here is defined as prepared digital materials stored as files. These files can be documents, audio, or video, but they're navigable, consumable content. They may be preloaded on the device, accessed via the mobile web, or downloaded or streamed on demand, but they're controlled only in presentation; other than that, they are not interacted with.

Of the channels typically available, two that are specific to cell phones should be considered. The first is simple messaging system (SMS), or text messages, which is typically limited to 140 characters. This channel is not a high-bandwidth mechanism, but it certainly can be used for short messages, such as briefly welcoming the learner, reactivating the concepts, providing microexamples, or providing feedback messages. With the ubiquity of text messaging, creative use of SMS could be a fun mechanism for learners.

Voice is a second alternative. Because minutes may be costly, this should be used with due caution, but learners could dial in for specific messages to a message system or receive a brief call or two, which would work best for introductions, examples, or summaries. Concepts might be somewhat more challenging, but a brief prose recitation might work. Listening to a quick story as an example could be worthwhile. Having the learner call in to a system and leave some course-related thoughts would also be a valuable reflective opportunity. As questions come up, learners could record and leave them.

Matching Media to Message

Overall, ideally we match the choice of communication media to the learning goal. If we need to present context, we use images (photos) or videos. If we want to restrict ourselves to the conceptual, we employ graphics or animation. For linguistic communication, we use text or speech (e.g., audio). For capturing dynamics of relationships, contextual or conceptual, video or animation, respectively, would be applicable, whereas for static relationships we can use images or graphics. Thus, a graphic of a steam plant might convey the underlying relationships of turbine to boiler, or an animation could demonstrate the water cycle within. However, when talking about building or repairing an actual example, a photo of the real one or a video of it running is suitable.

Table 5.1 Media Matching

	Static	Dynamic
Contextual	Photo	Video
Conceptual	Graphic	Animation
Linguistic	Text	Speech

From a purely technical perspective, of course, the device is largely unaware of whether a static image format is a photo or a graphic, although there are file formats that are significantly smaller if it is a graphic rather than an image. Similarly, an animation and a video both are represented in a dynamic visual format, and the device does not typically care. However, from a learning perspective, the distinction is important.

Diagrams and videos are both communication mechanisms that work particularly well for mobile devices. The conceptual relationships captured in a diagram are expressed in a concise way. Watching a video similarly can be accomplished easily on a mobile device. Small amounts of content can be usable, and of course audio can be very convenient. On the other hand, large amounts of text might be reserved for tablets.

One area that has been underexplored is the opportunity to use the comic strip (i.e., graphic novels or *manga*). Do not neglect the potential learning benefits of comic strips as a particular document format for performance support and learning. We have underused these powerful tools, which have a variety of valuable properties. Comics are a component of most current cultures, are easily processed, are low bandwidth, internationalize and localize easily (if the graphic treatments are sufficiently generic), strip away unnecessary context and allow for emphasizing concepts, and the thought bubbles provide a mechanism for metacognitive annotation.

This is a discussion of ideals, and there are various ways one format can be substituted for another. For example, many videos contain still images, audio narration, and more (think of Ken Burns's *Civil War*). And the dynamic nature of a video or animation can be conveyed by a sequence of still images or graphics.

Lectures

The obvious possibility is to capture lectures as delivered, via audio or combined with video, and this is in fact what has led to iTunes University, Apple's site for educational media files. Of course, an institution can handle this within its learning management system (LMS) or via its own portal as well. So, if the performance is already happening, whether in the lecture hall or classroom or via a webinar or virtual classroom tool, it can be captured, saved, and made available. Similarly, if a textbook or relevant readings or media materials (say, films or interviews) are already being used, making them available for mobile access is an obvious easy first step.

Grant Beever, then director of online services for Endeavour College, has gone further, creating lectures specifically for mobile delivery. He has teams create narrated presentations and then makes the audio, video, and slides available for download. This approach supports quality through the specific design for mobile delivery and flexibility through supporting a variety of formats.

Lectures and textbooks typically include introductions, concepts, and examples. These particularly make sense for tablet delivery but can make sense even on smartphones. Many institutions are making texts available on smartphones, for instance (Carter, 2009). Less capable devices may provide some barriers in quality of storage. And students are likely to be happy to have these materials available for whatever devices they possess: laptops, tablets, mobile phones, or any other device that can display media.

Custom

From there, start thinking about mobile-specific development and delivery. Here, it might be worth taking into account the delivery environment. While you *can* read long documents, watch long video, or listen to long audio, that's not the ideal role for mobile. When you go beyond *convenience* of access, mobile is really about quick access.

So, rather than reading a book, maybe having a rich diagram or set of diagrams would make sense. Or a summarized version of the text for review would be appropriate. Maybe a very focused animation could provide detailed illumination of the concepts—or, instead of a long video, a set of small videos at a sweet spot of perhaps 10 minutes. Similar to audio, small segments make more sense than long ones.

While students will be happy to have access to their materials also on a mobile device, any development investment should be focused on supplementing the course with small materials that may reactivate or elaborate on relevant materials, such as some additional representations of the concept.

Recent research suggests that content on a mobile device, at least mobile web, is twice as hard to consume successfully (Neilsen, 2011). Consequently, there are reasons to minimize the content developed and delivered for mobile consumption. Brevity is the soul not only of wit, as Shakespeare would have it, but also of mobile.

Learning Components

From a learning perspective, content is about the learning components of introductions, concepts, examples, and summaries. Each has unique properties, as identified in Chapter Three. Here we look at mobile options around those elements.

Introductions ideally open up the learner emotionally as well as activate relevant cognitive components. Emotions are brought in by drama or humor and can exaggerate the consequences positively for having the knowledge or skills or negatively for the lack thereof. A comic could achieve the humorous attempts and would work well for the potential bandwidth and screen limitations likely to be found on a mobile device. Dramatically, a video could achieve the same effect. Of course, prose is always an option.

Presenting concepts is about communicating the underlying idea. Here we might see diagrams to capture the relationships inherent in the core model or use animations to capture those relationships in a dynamic sense. We typically pair associated prose with diagrams or voice-overs with animations. These are rich representational opportunities for mobile delivery.

Presenting examples is really about capturing the story, telling the event starting with the initial situation, and then unfolding how the concept was applied, step by step (including backtracking and repair when appropriate), to yield a solution. This can be done with prose, but consider using a comic book or graphic novel approach (or even a comic strip). A narrated slide show or a video would work well. A voice recitation as a podcast is also worth considering if there is both a good story and storyteller, particularly if a portion of the audience commutes.

Summaries ideally would be customized, but in general recap what has been seen and point to new directions. An additional element is to close the emotional experience as well. There's nothing unique to mobile in most of this, though of course there could be links to further directions and greater depth. Brevity is desired, of course.

A uniquely mobile strategy for content is to consider smaller pieces more frequently. As mentioned in Chapter Three, the research on spaced learning suggests that this is not only more appropriate to the device but may also be more effective for learning. As a metaphor, think drip irrigation rather than flooding.

Context

The contextual opportunities for content are several-fold. For one, many examples of the principles likely already exist, but their relevance may not be obvious. The London Museum, for example, has an app that displays photos from history that exist in a person's current location (Museum of London, 2010).

One way of providing context-specific content is by tagging the environment. A web link can be placed at a location, either as text or using a quick-response (QR) code, as shown in Figure 5.1, a form of two-dimensional (2-D) image that most cell phone cameras can process. QR codes allow any text to be coded: for example, a message, a phone number, or a web link so that a picture of the image can cause the device to trigger an action. So, specific QR codes could be made that tag historical sites, architectural information, or other location-specific information such as geology or flora and can link to course-specific content.

In custom development on app devices, application programming interfaces (APIs) allow access to the hardware components of equipped devices. For example, the global positioning system (GPS) is accessible in this way, which provides one avenue to know where the user is. As a consequence, user locations can be tapped into to provide specifically relevant information.

Queries could also be made to a calendar to see what the user is currently doing or trigger events at particular times. So, if you knew a student had an assigned task at a particular time in an internship, you could provide preparation beforehand, support materials during, and evaluation rubrics or materials afterward.

Another opportunity is to design content to support specific performance, particularly for placements such as internships. Any paper-based support could be converted for mobile use, such as a map or a procedure. Already, flight checklists and medical support are being delivered on the iPad. Similarly, any of the support tools such as sidekicks and planners are relevant. You know the tasks the learner has to accomplish, but you may not know the specifics of where and when. You can do much more if you *do* know the specifics of where or when, whether from assignment to the learner or contextual clues such as GPS or calendar. So, for instance, you could provide support for specific tasks or locations if they were known, such as having a geology map available at a local park or architectural information in a historic section of town. Learners might access maps of various

Figure 5.1 QR Code.

features like demographic information and see how the manifestation of the neighborhood correlates.

A third opportunity is using real-world activity as a driver for interest in a topic. In this case, a meaningful activity such as a scavenger hunt or puzzle-solving game is designed that requires knowledge. Learners might follow a trail between locations linked by history, economy, or geography and use clues to find specific sites where they can then access relevant information. Now learners are motivated for the knowledge, and the issue is whether can they get it.

Meta-Learning

One of the characteristics of mobile is the ability to access information wherever and whenever. This can be powerful, but it comes with some consequences. We must continue to consider the sources of content and the quality of the results.

More pragmatically, we also must consider the ability to process information on a mobile form factor.

Being astute in querying for information and assessing the quality of the resulting data is not unique to mobile, but mobile adds to the importance. Typically, mobile access is contextualized in the moment, and consequently the time pressures may serve to preclude being as reflective as might be desirable. Learners, despite being more familiar with technology, cannot be assumed to possess astute information literacy (Open Education, 2008). A quick access context would exacerbate this. Providing support for comprehending good information access and information validation, particularly in a domain, would be a valuable consideration.

A second point is the ability to consume content of a variety of types on mobile devices. One is the technical issue of viewing whatever forms of media might be available, whether video, audio, or documents. Ensuring that learners are capable users of their devices ideally is not left to chance. A second issue is the ability to parse the representations used. This is not unique to mobile devices, but the particular form factors and navigation techniques to view large images may require some scaffolding.

Considering, and supporting, meta-learning skills is a useful contribution to learner success both in school and beyond.

MEDIA SPECIFICS

Documents

Documents are the most pervasive form of content: static text with graphics or images. From a learning perspective, documents can serve as introductions, concepts, examples, or summaries. In fact, most online learning content typically is document driven, from a digitized textbook to readings, diagrams, and more. The mobile advantage is that these materials can be pursued at convenient times when other activities are precluded (e.g., waiting in line or on a commute) and for reference in a relevant context.

An important principle for creating content, specifically documents for mobile, is to separate out the content from how it is displayed. You may have noticed how many (well-written) web pages will resize smoothly if you adjust the size of the browser window. This principle of design is particularly important when designing for delivery on a variety of mobile devices, where it goes beyond *just good practice* to critically important. And this holds true whether delivering to an application or mobile web. Do not specify fonts or sizes; allow the device to render as best for the output. eXtensible Markup Language (XML) is an improvement over HyperText Markup Language (HTML) for just this reason, and increasingly documents are being written in templates that support this separation. Darwin Integrate Topic Architecture (DITA), an XML standard for content, is worth investigating for just this reason.

In addition to considering the delivery representation, you should be considering the level of granularity at which you break up content. For reasons beyond mobile, specifically more flexible delivery (e.g., adaptive delivery), the goal is to separate individual examples from practice from concepts, and so on (Quinn, 2000). Do develop a rigorous tagging scheme as well, where the descriptors for the content objects you develop can be chosen programmatically rather than compiled by hand. Developing and describing a few extra concept representations, examples, and practice at development time initially supports reactivation over time with delivery at spaced intervals, whether mobile or desktop. The ability to access the different objects by description will support not only *pull* approaches by learners who want to choose what to review or have a short-term need but, going forward, also will support smart *push* or system-generated content (as will be discussed in Chapter Eight).

Another important consideration, specifically for images, is compression. High-quality images work great in print but are usually problematic on mobile devices. While this is changing, overall memory on mobile devices can be limited, and downloading content can be heavily impacted by file size. A similar but earlier approach to content structure was the XML-based DocBook standard, which had places for several sets of image for each one to be rendered on a device, including a high-quality one for print and a lower-quality one for the web. A third could be developed for mobile delivery. Although it is more and more common for mobile devices to make viewing large images manageable via scrolling, consideration of the necessity of a high-quality image versus a lower one for mobile viewing is a worthwhile investment of time.

The nice story with documents is that they are the proverbial *low-hanging fruit*. With little work, your suite of PDFs and slide presentations, for example, can be made available for viewing on mobile devices. Most of the tools you use have output or export functions to create file types that likely can be viewed on mobile devices. Creating a mobile portal for these is one way to empower an organization.

Audio and Video

Audio and video, when well done, can be quite engaging. As dynamic content, they present a continual stream of content. Both can be used to present introductions and examples. Audio can convey concepts, but the lack of visual accompaniment may limit the applicability to content with multiple relationships, as the linear media combined with human working memory limits make it somewhat difficult. Video can work for all purposes.

Examples, in particular, are highly suited to the use of dynamic media. Stories are powerful ways to communicate the flow of problem solving, showing the application of concepts to context. The dynamic media can be compelling whether it is a storyteller telling the story or a visual narration of the situation. The ability to access additional examples conveniently is a powerful mobile adjunct to formal learning.

Video is a particularly powerful media, capturing as it does our highly developed visual system, and, typically coupled with an audio track, can be very engaging. When poorly done, however, the result can be almost aversive.

Audio also has the property of nondirection: that is, audio can be perceived without being oriented toward the direction of production. Thus, visual attention can be on the road or on a task, and the audio can be anywhere within hearing. Visual, on the other hand, requires a person to look in a particular direction to perceive the signal.

Audio and video are dynamic content, content that one must pay attention to; if your attention wavers, you may lose your place. A good principle of design is providing a way to replay and, if the selection is more than a few seconds, giving ways to control playback including pause and play, and moving within.

Dynamic content, like document images, also has trade-offs in size and quality. Mobile formats err on the side of small size to minimize download times and costs. Redundant files for viewing on the desktop and mobile are not unreasonable.

ACCESSING

Making content available for mobile access is typically a two-part process. The first component is creating the media in a mobile-deliverable format. The second component is making the mobile content accessible.

Documents can be served out as PDF files, as web pages, or in raw text. A newer development is the e-book and associated e-reader. This takes the traditional prose of a book and makes it available to read on a mobile device. Books are increasingly available not only in print but also for consuming on mobile devices.

Dedicated readers like the Sony eReader, Amazon Kindle, and Barnes & Noble Nook are increasingly being challenged by e-reader apps on mobile platforms like tablets and smartphones, including apps for Kindle and Nook. Many textbooks are already available as e-books, and most fiction and nonfiction printed by the publishers are also being made accessible for online purchase.

A variety of formats are still offered. In addition to raw text, many readers can read common document formats like Adobe's PDF and the relatively new e-pub format for e-books. Amazon has its own proprietary format, while Barnes & Noble, Apple, and Sony are using the e-pub format with a digital rights management scheme to protect purchased content. Writing into an XML format increases the likelihood that content can be easily transferred into an e-book format; thus, not only textbooks but also personal documents will be available in the e-reader formats. Calibre is a free, open-source, and cross-platform tool that allows content to be organized and published in a variety of e-reader formats, whereas Sigil is a complementary, free, open-source, and cross-platform what-you-see-is-what-you-get (WYSIWYG) e-book editor.

Many smartphones and tablets can display both PDFs and e-books and also Microsoft Office formats (a common document format in organizations). While most traditional cell phones, however, are restricted to SMS and mobile web, the more capable smartphone is on the rise.

Audio and video can exist in a variety of formats. Formats like MP3 or Advanced Audio Coding (AAC) for audio and MP4 or 3GP (multimedia file format of the 3rd Generation Partnership Project, 3GPP) for video are fairly universal now. Unfortunately, format barriers still remain, with various players with vested interests supporting different standards. And the standards evolve. The best advice is to look for the format advice at the time you are ready to host content to a platform. For learners who own Apple's iconic devices, whether iPod, iPhone, or iPad, these are a powerful distribution mechanism.

Educationally speaking, one obvious delivery mechanism is Apple's iTunes University. For years now, it has been a way for educational institutions to archive and make accessible audio and video recordings of lectures. Beyond the core personal information management (PIM) applications, one of the first higher education applications of mobile technology was listening to lectures on an iPod. The 2010 Campus Computing report indicates that capturing lectures is a growing component of university strategy.

Grant Beever, mentioned earlier, uses iTunes University to support the downloading of lectures. The audio and video files are available through iTunes, as his research demonstrated that most of his audience had access or was able to get it. Of roughly 3,000 full-time students and 10,000 taking at least one course, 1,500 downloads a week occur.

In general, conversion of documents into a variety of formats is now built into most content creation tools. In addition, a variety of free and open-source conversion tools is available for many formats on the main platforms.

Hosting content is the second component of mobile delivery. The devices need a way to access the content. Accessing it through the web, via a portal, and having it downloaded is one option. Synching it onto the device is a second. A wide range of mobile interfaces to content and learning management systems is making the hosting more automatic.

Some platforms are also specifically mobile delivery mechanisms.

LMS

Given that the LMS is a common component of the campus infrastructure, it is worth briefly surveying the current content delivery status of its major platforms.

Blackboard's Mobile Learn platform provides access to the resources hosted in its LMS via mobile devices. At the time of writing, it has developed apps for iPhone and iPad, Android, and Blackberry. These allow access to the content, such as PDF and Microsoft Office documents, as well as media files.

Desire2Learn's mobile solution for Blackberry currently supports access of only textual content.

Active development is also under way for Moodle, the premier open-source higher education LMS. iOS apps already exist, and Android is in development. Both should be available by the time you read this.

It appears that Sakai, another open-source LMS, has mobile in development at the time of writing.

SUMMARY

Content, along with administrative services, is the easy first step for mobile. Many universities are capturing lectures almost instantly now, and textbooks and LMS content are becoming almost automatically available.

The next step is to look to more meaningful interactions, both computer based and social. We'll look at the former before we look to the latter.

PRACTICE

1. What content do you have already that can be made mobile accessible?

2. What changes can you and do you need to make to build mobile formats as an automatic outcome of your development processes?

CONTENT FORM

You can use this form to spark your thinking.

	Introduction	Concept	Example	Summary
Document				
Audio				
Video				

For example:

	Introduction	Concept	Example	Summary
Document	A comic exaggerating the consequences of not being able to do Y	A diagram	A graphic novel version of someone solving a problem using the concept, with annotation	A short but sweet reconnection of the learning content back to the larger context; acknowledgment of the learner's effort and new accomplishments; and pointers to what's next.
Audio	Character X doesn't know how to do Y, and ends up in trouble as a consequence	An eloquent presentation of the concept	A well-told story of a problem, applying the concept (ideally, with some false starts) ending in triumph	A congratulations message from the instructor acknowledging the effort and the new capabilities of the learner.
Video	An introduction to the topic by a well-known and eloquent "name" in the field	An animation of the underlying concept	A documentary-style story of how the concept was applied in a particular situation	A video capturing the learner's new capabilities as they play out in the real world and connecting the learner to the topic.

6

Practice: Interactivity and Assessment

Key point: Have learners make meaningful decisions.

As indicated in Chapter Three, practice is really the core to making learning that is effective: that is, both retained and transferrable to appropriate situations. This requires ensuring that there are meaningful objectives, but this leads to a real chance for impact.

mLearning plays a role by not only bringing convenience but also making practice available in the particular situation of the classroom. The *compute* capability is critical, but, as this chapter shows, *capture* will also be able to play a role.

DESIGN

The core of meaningful practice is application. Making the choices in practice that need to be made *after* the learning experience is the best preparation, and preparatory practice is part of the path. While there is some recitation of knowledge in most university learning, meaningful application is still less than prevalent. We largely want to focus on making the decisions and applying the cognitive skills that characterize real performance.

The issue is balance between the knowledge that learners need to know and application of that knowledge to solve problems. It is easy to test the former and typically harder to assess the latter. Yet the latter is the more important ultimate outcome and is the task that most engages the learner. The ideal situation is when a search for knowledge is driven by a realized need that develops while trying to achieve meaningful goals. As a consequence, here the emphasis is largely on meaningful tasks. Technology gives us tools to make more meaningful tasks, and mobile technologies help us more flexibly deliver meaningful tasks as well as knowledge tests.

Note that I do not make a big distinction between formative and summative assessment. If learners get feedback about how they did and what it means (and they should), it is formative assessment. If a score is recorded, the assessment is summative. All assessment should be formative (why miss an opportunity for learning?), and truly the only summative assessment to care about is whether learners can ultimately perform to the desired level. Others will have different views.

There may well be a concern that unproctored performance may be suspect. If learners can take assessment anywhere, they may be assisted. Two factors play into this, as there are two sorts of assistance. One is where the user has access to resources like references. Increasingly, we recognize that we should allow learners to not have to memorize information they can look up. On the other hand, however, if someone else is taking the assessment, we have a more legitimate concern that we are not assessing the appropriate individual. In some sense, that punishes the learner more than the institution, but it is an understandable desire to align individual with performance. As mobile devices increasingly include cameras for video conferencing, we may be able to combine a video of the user while assessing, but for now we will need to have other authentication measures or not have any summative assessment performed out of the classroom.

Processing

An important component here is thinking about the processing that is being accomplished. Elements that contribute to meaningful processing include personalization, extension, and application.

By personalization, in this instance, we are talking specifically about having learners relate a concept to their own past or intended experience. By applying a concept to explain things in the past or to think about how it would be useful in the future, learners are exercising the relationships in the concept. Thus, having learners keep a journal of such personalizations is a valuable exercise.

A second form of processing the relationships is to have learners extend the concept by considering how other concepts affect the current content focus. Again, learners are exploring the concept. For example, learners might be asked how an economic concept such as supply and demand might play out in a different type of economy or how a medical concept might apply under different environmental conditions. The point is to find a way to have learners reprocess the concept.

The ultimate form of processing to achieve the purposes of retention and transfer is applying the concepts to a context. Here, we characterize the context with a story and then create a situation that requires a decision, an application of the knowledge (Quinn, 2005). This can even be just a better written multiple-choice question, but scenarios and simulations are richer ways to develop understanding, particularly if deep practice is required because of complexity and variability.

Assessment

The principle with assessment is to align the task to the desired outcome. Ideally, as indicated already, some objective criteria determine the final performance, and the tasks are aligned to that. A criterion-referenced model rather than normative performance (e.g., grading on a curve) is desired.

Mobile assessment provides several benefits. The first is to evaluate on the fly, while instruction is occurring, to customize the learning experience. The second is to provide regular checks during the larger learning experience, the overall course, to help learners track how they are doing as well as for the instructor to assess progress.

These assessments likely need both knowledge tests, which measure whether learners have the requisite preparation, and application, which assures learners' ability to perform. Reactivation of this knowledge helps guarantee retention over time, and increasing the suite of contexts seen across examples and practice supports transfer to all appropriate situations.

Considerations

A number of principles come into play when designing interactive experiences. Particularly for mobile, we want to consider a variety of factors. We want to ensure we're keeping the design simple, navigable, and accessible.

Interactions are, at the core, the presentation of a choice to the learner, the learner's response, and, ideally, feedback to the learner. Any of the available means the device provides for communicating the context and outcomes to users and for users to communicate their choice of action back to the system will work. There have been successful examples of interactions via text message, navigable text or web pages, and of course custom applications.

The ability, however, to track and report learner responses as part of the learner record is an issue that is still evolving. Apps, either web or custom, can be written to write to learner management system (LMS) application programming interfaces (APIs), but this requires nontrivial development skills. Increasingly, LMSs provide mobile delivery of their existing content, and tools now produce standards-compliant reporting, so this problem is on the way out, at least for standard forms of interactions (e.g., multiple-choice questions). Still, the capability of mobile–LMS integration is still idiosyncratic, and, as a consequence, mobile practice can be the most challenging of areas in which to engage.

An alternative is to have responses sent to the instructor for evaluation. Any of the available communication channels could be used, including e-mail, text messages, microblog responses, edits into a collaborative workspace, or more. None of this is unique to mobile, but the flexibility is useful even though the requirement of manual marking is still present.

Despite recent screen size increases on mobile devices, the physical constraints on device size for portability and on the ability of our eyes to consume information of decreasing size mean that we must consider some limitations on the available screen real estate and focus on streamlining the visual display. The principles of minimalism play a role here, in that the focus should be on communicating *telegraphically*, using a spare style to convey the context. One lesson learned is that full sentences are not necessary in many instances and that communicative phrases will suffice. Using terse prose satisfies multiple constraints including bandwidth and limited interfaces. It's helpful to think about the least that can be done to achieve the desired goal.

For example, in a mobile case study presented in *mLearning* (Metcalf, 2006), a quiz and some mini-scenarios were created for a negotiation course based on the instructor's prose. It took two passes to reduce the prose sufficiently to work effectively on seven lines by fifteen characters of text. The requirement was to abandon any attempt to maintain proper sentences and to instead focus on communication with a minimum of text.

Another important issue, particularly for interactive content, is navigation. Smaller interfaces make it harder to communicate the content as well as available options and the current location in the information space. Careful attention to clues and consistency of interface actions are necessary. Consistency is one form of support; so if there are platform consistencies in how to navigate or if users will have previous experience with another relevant application, take advantage of the mechanisms already known to minimize confusion. Providing location clues like a *breadcrumb trail*, which is the simple list often seen on web pages that tells you which pages you've navigated through (for example, if this book were a site, this location might be *The Mobile Academy > Chapter 6 > Design > Considerations*), is a familiar mechanism that users will be able to take advantage of.

Ensure that the information architecture is sufficiently communicated to minimize problems with learners getting lost. User testing is important. Expert review will help remove some problems, but user experience is the ultimate needed outcome. Good information architecture makes certain that information is located where the user expects and that the user can make good inferences about how to proceed. Ideally, however, the interactions are small and simple enough that navigation isn't an issue, and response options are clear.

INTERACTIONS

There are several chronological variations in how mobile interactions can proceed. Asynchronous interactions are ones that learners access at their convenience. Then there can be timed interactions, such as simulations or games. More advanced versions of this will come into play in Chapter Eight when we talk about advanced topics. Synchronous interactions are accessed live during either a face-to-face (F2F) or online course. F2F courses in particular can use mobile devices as tools for interactions.

Audience response systems are known tools for collecting data from audiences, and there are solutions that use cell phones or smartphone apps to accomplish this task. Asking questions during a live session can allow learners to anonymously indicate their understanding and thus faculty to customize the course. So, a question could be posed in class asking students to respond. A web interface that they can access from their phones would give them the chance to go to the page and respond, while the web page could display the results. Polls can also be taken that allow learners to see what others think.

Tools now exist for audience response systems. A simple online search will help reveal the possibilities. An alternative could be the development of a web form (a web-based fill-in page that posts the information entered back to a server for processing; think of the way data like home address are entered into a web page) that is mobile web accessible.

The next level is *quizzes*, composed of true–false, multiple-choice, and short-answer questions. Quizzes typically assess knowledge but can also capture more meaningful situated performance. Informal methods could be adequate, where questions could be sent to a microblog with a hash tag for the course and responses sent directly to the instructor. E-mail and text messages similarly can be used. For formal recording to an LMS, tools would be needed that can report to the LMS, whether they are system-provided ones or external ones that produce compatible learning objects.

Ideally, learners will be cast in a role setting up a story and then will be given a particular situation where they have to act and then see the consequences of that choice. Doing this requires conveying a context and providing a means of action on the part of the learner.

So, for example, the negotiation miniscenarios mentioned above set up a story, such as "you are in this role, and you have this need, with a customer with this relationship." A situation would then occur such as "you open your negotiation this way, and they do that." The learner would have several response choices; in this case, the model for negotiation used had five ways to respond: ignore, confront soft, confront hard, try humor, or walk away. After the learner responded, he'd receive feedback on that approach and on the outcome.

This approach can work with anything from a simple question, properly constructed, to a serious game. Naturally, there are associated trade-offs in development costs as well. Each medium has its own characteristics, though really most any tool can be put to almost any use. The more complex the interaction, the more constraints exist and the more complex environments are required.

Most traditional questions—true–false, multiple-choice, and fill-in-the-blank—can be developed and delivered with simple tools. Web forms will work for these and are the easiest solution. Some tools can take web forms and save them as applications, though they are not necessary. The issue is in designing good questions rather than in being able to deliver them, and well-developed multiple-choice questions can serve as mini-scenarios, with the question stem holding both the story setting and the particular situation and the different responses representing different courses of action.

More and more, the LMS vendors provide the ability for learners to access quizzes on their mobile devices. Similarly, the ancillary or companion materials that publishers provide to supplement their textbooks increasingly are or will be available for mobile access. Further, there are stand-alone tools that allow instructors to create and share self-evaluation. These mechanisms let learners test their knowledge to their own level of confidence.

Hardwiring the relationships among questions, so that one choice prompts a different next question than another choice, is the basis of a branching scenario. These are easily implemented as web pages, though they can also be put into action as applications. Branching scenarios can also be implemented in presentation software, which can be output as e-learning (likely to move away from Flash to HTML5) and consequently also potentially as a mobile application.

I distinguish among simulations, scenarios, and games like this:

- A *simulation* is technically just a model of a system, can be in any state the system can be in, and can be moved to any other state by appropriate actions. Self-motivated and effective learners can discover what they need from a simulation, but these are usually not safe assumptions.

- A *scenario* is a simulation that has been put into an initial state, and the learner is asked to achieve a goal state. Typically, we wrap a story around this to make the actions and goal meaningful.

- We can *tune* a scenario into a *game* if we adjust the interactions until the level of challenge and feedback lead to a subjectively compelling experience—not just fun, but *hard fun*. That is, we *turn* it into a game by tuning.

The distinction made when discussing branching scenarios is really just an implementation detail. Branching scenarios hard-code the consequences of choices in particular links. The alternative situation is where a simulation calculates the consequences. While the latter does take some more explication of the actual relationships, the benefit is the ability to add some variability and adaptivity and generate almost infinite replay. This facilitates covering lots of contexts or a range of difficulty to achieve sufficient practice to truly master a skill. Business simulations are a classic case, where the effects on profitability of costs, pricing, marketing, competition, and more can be calculated so that students can try to run a business successfully.

The ultimate form of deep practice is a simulation-driven scenario, ideally tuned into a game. The requirements of processing, however, may tax a mobile device's capabilities. Rich games are being developed for mobile devices, which suggests that capabilities exist but that the development costs in most cases exceed the budget for a particular course. This will change, but as mentioned in Chapter Two uncertainty still exists in the market over what path will prevail. Increasingly, however, we will see publishers and others producing mobile-delivered simulations, and the ability to practice when and where convenient and when inspiration strikes may be valuable.

Another alternative is server-side processing, so that the mobile interface is just a front end to the computational power existing on a server somewhere. This appears to be the case in the University of Aberdeen's simple messaging system (SMS) simulation on managing floods, though the underlying architecture was a branching simulation.

However, on an editorial note, I do *not* consider tarted-up drill-and-kill to be a real game. While it is useful for when knowledge needs to be memorized, we too often resort to knowledge tests when more meaningful objectives should be established. Putting fancy production values on meaningless activity is still meaningless activity.

The goal is to have learners map the conceptual models to the simulated world and explore the models' ability to explain occurrences, predict outcomes, and form the basis of decisions. Model-based reasoning is important, and simulated worlds are the way to explore and apply the models.

The mobile argument is to support spacing practice out and convenience of access. If learners can practice meaningfully, they stand a greater chance of retaining the information over time and transferring to all appropriate situations. Particularly for tablets, when longer interactions are needed, the intimacy and convenience may make for lasting skill improvement. Systems may allow scheduled distribution, but if using informal methods the instructor can distribute as desired.

Naturally, feedback on performance is needed. When the performance is contextualized (and this is to be encouraged), the scenario should have the experience closed before external feedback ensues. And, of course, the feedback should link the learner's performance in context back to the concept.

Context

Just as with context-sensitive content, we can also consider context-specific practice. Professionals do not work in a vacuum but typically apply their skills in particular locations.

Learners can be given location-specific or context-specific particular challenges to work on, and these can be delivered and captured via mobile devices. The opportunities for contextualized tasks are still just being explored, but the possibilities are intriguing; some ideas are explored in Chapter Eight.

One such example, conducted as an experiment, had learners carrying a tablet from anatomy station to anatomy station and filling out questionnaires that used to be paper based (Jalali, Trottier, Tremblay, & Hincke, 2011). Such an approach is indicative of the type of location-specific assessment that could be conducted. This could be via web forms, a built-in tool, or a custom application. The advantage of this approach is that the data can be automatically collected and even marked before the learner leaves (providing more timely feedback), as well as other programmatic benefits such as randomized questions or response options, adaptive assessment, and more.

Another opportunity is to have learners perform a virtual task in an appropriate context. The learner could play a site-specific role in a particular location, such as a geologist at a natural site or medical personnel in a hospital. Specific tasks could be performed and information displayed on the device that would advance a story, allowing the learner to gather data and make decisions. This would likely require a preprogrammed system or someone playing game master running the game in the background.

Capture

As presaged at the beginning of the chapter, a unique capability of mobile devices comes with their ability to capture. This plays out in a couple of ways. For one, learners can go out and capture instances of the concept in context, whether with audio, images, or video. This can be as an assignment in and of itself or merely learners' way to illustrate points in their assignments. For instance, a learner could capture a picture of a particular plant or building, a recording of an interview, or a video of a performance for discussion with other learners or an instructor.

An important way for learners to capture their understandings is by representing them. Having learners write their thoughts is an important opportunity. Whether external processing occurs as quick thoughts expressed via microblogs or longer posts, it is important. Moreover, having learners annotate their products and performances, making their thinking visible, is important for the ability to comprehend and provide feedback. Mobile tools to support microblogging, blogging, and word processing exist and support such capture. Of course, e-mail for discussion lists and web access to other writing tools such as cloud-based documents also can be used.

Software also is available that can either record audio or transform voice to text. Voice memo software or audio recording can chronicle quick thoughts for later transcription. More, dictation software exists that transcribes speech with increasing accuracy. So learners can increasingly capture thoughts when they occur and have them available for later processing.

Learners can also capture their own performances, whether directly by the previously listed methods (recording their own voice attempts at language or videoing their dance) or by measuring or inputting outputs of their performance (e.g., filling out forms with the results they achieved or having mentors enter evaluations). These can be brought back for self-evaluations and comment or instructor feedback. These stored performances can also serve as components of a portfolio to be coupled with other work products. Having learners perform or create and then annotate a version with their reflections and underlying thought processes involved in the creation or performance provides a valuable tool for evaluation of their thinking and begins to develop literacies beyond text, an important 21st-century skill.

Another form of capture is to use applications to gather contextual data. I had the opportunity to observe Professor John Ittelson as he prepared a presentation on how a pitch pipe and audio oscillator software could be used to demonstrate scientific concepts. The software would process and graph the audio generated by the pitch pipe (or any other sound source). Rich computational tools exist, including calculators and many domain-specific tools, to support extending the learning experience. Many of the instruments that used to be expensive in laboratories now run as applications on mobile platforms or are coupled to these mobile devices via hardware that can be lower cost due to the lack of need of powerful computational capabilities as these are provided by the mobile device. The availability of such software and the portability of the devices make fieldwork more plausible.

It could be a powerful extension if learners capture data from the world relevant to their studies. For instance, they could capture temperatures, soil samples, geologic information, fauna, flora, or any other types of information relevant to the topic at hand. Looking for instances of pertinent information reactivates the knowledge and contextualizes it as well as makes it personal. An extension to this appears in the next chapter.

Increasingly in the corporate space, it is easy for companies to buy software that allows employees to upload and share videos or capture their own desktop and demonstrate software. Public tools include YouTube. These capabilities, whether built into the software infrastructure being used or via publicly available software, allow learners to record or create video and audio files. The benefit to this, as mentioned already, is that it allows rich forms of representation and annotation, a new media literacy, to be supported.

Ittelson is active in the e-portfolio area and pointed me to an iPhone app created by the University of Minnesota and aptly named *ePortfolio for iPhone*. This tool is specifically designed to support uploading photos to the University of Minnesota ePortfolio System to be incorporated in learners' aggregate e-portfolios.

Similarly, DoubleTake for Purdue is a video capture and sharing mobile application for use at the university. It allows learners to upload and view video.

META-LEARNING

The ability to take assessments where convenient and to have richer forms of capture and representation provide some interesting consequences going forward for learning. Self-monitoring, context effects, and more become important considerations.

If there are context-specific performances, learners need to understand the nature of how context affects performance. In real performance away from the learning experience, there are likely consequences different from the ones experienced in the learning experience. While good simulation design can mimic those contexts, some differences will be necessary. Providing reflection questions on context can assist learners in understanding the implications.

Context-independent practice, performed at the learner's convenience, still has context consequences too. The specific context in which learners perform will similarly have effects. Helping learners understand context effects to comprehend the consequences is valuable here as well.

Performing without supervision means that there are missed opportunities for monitoring performance separate from what is assessed in the task. Preparation, systematicity, and more are issues in achieving success. Assisting learners in understanding and internalizing self-monitoring capabilities can be a valuable contribution to their development.

SUMMARY

The most important support for learning is meaningful activity, and thus practice is critical. While it does not *have* to be mobile delivered, the ability to space practice out and to allow learners the flexibility to practice when and where they want provides both better outcomes and happier learners.

In addition, the ability to use the unique capabilities of their devices—audio or video capture—provides new opportunities not only to support learning but also to develop new skills as well.

Of course, while practice alone is valuable, practice with others has unique advantages. It is time to look at social media, which is the topic of the next chapter.

PRACTICE

1. What tools already exist in your location or institution that can generate practice? Can you go beyond just knowledge test?

2. What additional tools do you need to deliver mobile interactives at a high level?

3. How can you support learners in creating and sharing media files?

CATEGORY CHECKLIST

This list considers the categories of possible practice:

- Personal reflection/text: web form/blog, platform tool, custom app
- Quiz: web form, platform tool, custom app
- Branching scenario: web pages, converted presentation, custom app
- Simulation-driven interaction: custom app
- Context-specific tasks
- Capture: audio, images, video, text

7

Going Social

Key point: Get learners interacting around the concepts.

To this point, we have largely been talking about individual learning, but social learning is powerful both formally and informally. As I have previously noted (Quinn, 2009b), "Working together helps unearth different views of what's happening, and allows negotiation of shared understanding." In that negotiation, there is the opportunity for powerful learning.

We have seen how *content* delivers learning resources such as textbooks and media files and how *capture* and *compute* play a role in practice activities to apply the knowledge; now social learning is the fourth C: *communicate*. Mobile tools facilitate interaction, supporting not only convenient access but also coordination and communication regardless of location.

The tools for communication are increasing. Microblogging started with Twitter, but now more tools incorporate the equivalent functionality (e.g., Yammer). Wiki tools and Google Docs have become mainstream. Social networks like MySpace and Facebook now have corporate equivalents. This is on top of existing social tools such as e-mail and phones. These capabilities are increasingly appearing in learning management systems (LMSs) as well, and they provide rich learning opportunities.

The dimension of synchrony is important here. Synchronous communication allows addressing the moment of need. Asynchronous communication, however, can be more reflective (Quinn, Mehan, Levin, & Black, 1983). Each has its role. Clarifying questions during a presentation can keep learning on track. Taking time to reflect and contribute over time can develop deeper understanding. On the other hand, inappropriate interruptions might derail a message, and taking too long might mean a missed opportunity. Choosing the right medium for the message consequently is an important issue.

LEARNING INTERACTIONS

In learning, there are two types of social interactions: learner–instructor and learner–learner. In the former case, there is little new added by mobile except the convenience of communicating when and where desired. More generally, instructors can pass on information about upcoming assignments, provide unique feedback about assignments, and answer questions.

The augmented classroom, real or virtual, has now come to pass. Much of the virtual classroom software has mobile interfaces for participation, so Adobe's Connect, Citrix's GoToMeeting, and Cisco's WebEx all have smartphone clients, allowing more flexibility in learners interacting with instructors. And the capabilities of virtual classrooms, such as chats and polls, are accessible via mobile tools in the real classroom; the same principles apply to both, such as checking understanding on an anonymous basis and supporting learner questions, which increases engagement.

One alternative to the regular learner–instructor interaction that can be unique to mobile is when connection can happen in context. In addition to learner-initiated connection for, say, an after-action review, a possibility would be a proactive connection made upon an external trigger such as task completion or at some other signal event. So, for instance, after a task in an internship such as a site inspection, an instructor could be connected to the learner to inquire about the event and ascertain the learner's progress. This would require custom programming, however.

Real power in social learning comes from learner–learner interaction. As mentioned in Chapter Three, social constructivism tells us that when learners are given assignments to collaborate, they express their various understandings, review the differences, reprocess the requirements, and continually engage with the concept to achieve a shared understanding.

The valuable processing that happens when reflecting personally or extending or applying a concept is magnified in social interactions. When learners reflect publicly and read other reflections, more processing is happening. When groups debate a response to an association extension, the processing cycles are tighter; when they work together to solve problems, the dialogue is richer.

Some requirements optimize the outcomes. The right size groups help, as does the right degree of ambiguity in the assignment to foster productive discussion. Dyads have proved useful in performance tasks: one person interacts while another makes more strategic decisions. Teams of more than five can become unmanageable. Variety in teams supports a richer interaction. Nothing yet is unique to mobile, but it is worth repeating the principles.

Also, do not assume that learners know how to work well together. Learners benefit from explicit guidance on how you expect them to work together and your expectations for their contributions. Guidelines such as individually offering thoughts before evaluating group contributions help ensure that all group members are engaging their intellect. Mobile participation can have unique issues, such as appropriate times to communicate and appropriate forms of communication. Texts or calls in the wee hours of the night may be problematic for both instructors and learners.

Existing mechanisms, such as discussion forums via e-mail, can now be interacted with when desired or convenient and are great tools for extending concepts. You can ask everyone to put out their thoughts and to contribute constructively on another post. New tools such as wikis and collaborative web-hosted documents can also be accessed when convenient when mobile-web accessible. Assignments to make joint responses to requests for proposals (RFP), for example, allow the RFP to constrain the task and mimic real-world jobs and require teams to collaborate to interpret the task and create a shared response. The important point is to find a way to have learners interact productively. These are not unique to mobile, but mobile supports new access and the potential for context-specific components.

We can also hold office hours with synchronous communication tools, and mobile versions increase the likelihood of participation and may make it easier for faculty as well as learners. Some may prefer conference calls, others may prefer chats, and video conferencing may also be feasible. Mobile increases the potential for inclusion.

Parallel conversations, too, can be seen. Learners can be allowed to use a channel such as a tweet stream or other mechanism to have a simultaneous conversation during a presentation. While it might seem risky to allow ongoing dialogue, the fact is that it can happen anyway, so making it public and exploiting it makes much sense.

For example, an instructor could provide a hash tag for a class, and the students could tweet during the lecture. The instructor can monitor the tweetstream while presenting, and this allows the learners to ask questions and interact without disturbing the presentation. This is very much like the chat window in a virtual classroom, but it is brought back to the real classroom. Learners can participate by responding to the instructor's questions, and vice versa, as well as each other's comments. This may prove difficult for an instructor to manage or feel comfortable with, but folks are using such tools successfully. With practice, you can check and see what learners are thinking and when their thinking is going awry.

Communication is not just language; images, audio, and video can also be shared and commented on. This can be as assigned or as individual contributions to a group project. Learners can discuss shared content, can dialogue around individual assignments, or can work together to create collaborative artifacts. Learners can capture pictures that illustrate (or contradict) concepts, can shoot videos of themselves performing tasks, or can even cocreate a video that represents their understanding of a particular situation and share it with others. Other organizations are creating their own solutions, whether programming, using commercial software, or finding the capability in their existing systems.

It's about deeper learning, though nonlearning socialization is not to be dismissed. Communication can also be about coordinating, making arrangements, as well as establishing oneself as an individual with other interests as well.

Context Specific

Beyond the convenience of communicating when the mood strikes, as mobile supports, a second benefit can be seen where the assignment is *in situ*, that is, when the learners are at appropriate locations for specific activities or are together and can engage in technology-enhanced activities.

While we can assign collaborative tasks that mimic the way learners might actually have to perform as professionals, we can augment those situations with mobile tools. Thus, the type of online role plays that unfold via e-mail, for instance (Wills, Leigh, & Ip, 2011), could be run face to face, and although the character information could be made mobile, new information could be introduced to one actor via a mobile tool that is different from what another might receive. Learners might perform social tasks such as emergency responders, medical personnel, or any location-specific group task in context. Information available via mobile tools could simulate what learners actually might discover in the location, according to the role each is playing. We will revisit this in the next chapter.

Learners can, of course, use their mobile tools to create shared representation while colocated as well. Learners can collaborate to create audio or video files, for instance, presenting a viewpoint or raising an issue. Coupling instructor observation with tool-captured records of actions would provide rich insight into the learning process.

Another opportunity, building on the idea in the previous chapter on capturing relevant data, is to aggregate data across learners. Learners can discuss how the data varied according to, for example, location or time, and the patterns can be mapped and graphed. Inferences from the data can be a powerful source of discussion about causation and other important relationships in conceptual understanding. The mechanism for collection, of course, would be dependent on the data desired.

SOCIAL MEDIA

The most common forms of mobile communication are one to one: simple messaging system (SMS) (i.e., text messaging) or voice. However, in the case of internet connectivity and web access, more possibilities exist for communication. E-mail is a well-known example, and then there are all the new data-enabled social media tools.

New social media capabilities include what Brent Schlenker, eLearn dev blogger and corporate eLearning strategy consultant, has called the five "-ables" of social media (Schlenker, 2009). Social media should be:

- *Feedable* (or *subscribable*), capable of being syndicated out to and followed by others
- *Searchable* so that others can find it
- *Linkable* so others can point to it

- *Taggable* so others can add value to it

- *Editable* so others can improve it

The focus is on ensuring that anything created can be added to, shared, followed, and more. Mobile tools can support all these capabilities and can allow a virtuous cycle of learning, creating, and providing feedback.

More possibilities exist when distance learners might be able to visit some appropriate venue near their locations (e.g., a hospital) and have a venue-specific presentation (e.g., a discussion about hospital administration). Learners could discuss the local situation they experience and compare notes. By considering the learning concepts in context, they are processing them in valuable ways.

Instant messaging (IM) allows more than one person to have a conversation, creating a text chat capability. Skype acts as several types of tools, including IM, but also supports voice through voice over internet protocol (VoIP) and even video conferencing.

Microblogging is a relatively new capability and shares the form factor of a text message with the subscription capabilities of a blog. Twitter is one microblogging tool, though some packages may have their own form.

Tools such as blogs and wikis can support mobile access either through dedicated apps or web interfaces. Similarly, media repositories that allow posting of images, videos, bookmarks, or presentations can be mobile accessible, so Flickr, YouTube, Delicious, and SlideShare and their equivalents can be considered. The mobile benefit is in sharing media, or accessing it, when inspiration strikes or when examples exist rather than when conveniently at a desktop computer. Similarly, the opportunity is to see what others have said when they contribute, not when they are tethered.

Integrated social media networks, such as Facebook, typically include a suite of tools from the set of, for example, blogs, wikis, discussion forums, and media repositories. They add the ability to provide an individual profile and link directly to other people and aggregate a variety of media. They also let folks form groups and interact around topics of interest. As such, they provide a way for groups to be created to discuss topics and share work as well as to collaborate. Also, both public tools like LinkedIn and Facebook and their proprietary versions provide mobile interfaces.

Trade-offs are involved in using public versus proprietary tools. Learners already active in social networks might prefer not having to go to a different environment to do coursework. On the other hand, security in a vendor-supplied tool may be higher, and free tools have been known to suddenly change requirements (as Ning did when it phased out free accounts).

Regardless of what tool is used, learners may choose certain ones to form their own study groups, whereas instructors can use networks for their coursework to post syllabi and tools like media repositories and wikis for assignments including creating a presentation, document, or video, having a discussion on a topic, or combining the two to share and have associated discussions. For instance, learners could perform and capture the performance on video to share with the class and discuss.

One advantage to using a more general tool than the social networking associated with a traditional course-focused LMS is to build a community of individuals interested in the topic to extend the learning experience for the graduates and provide support for the new learners. Thus, alumni of a course could gather and share tips, which would provide a demonstration for the learners of how this knowledge is put into practice. Such a community could be a valuable source of posteducation employment, feedback to the program, and more.

Context may also play a role; for one, learners might be able to search for someone else taking their subject who is nearby (and has allowed such contact). Context-specific group activities such as a group field trip might also be assigned or at least available. Collaborative tasks might be assigned that are allocated to a specific location.

Jane Bozarth, in her book *Social Media for Trainers* (2010), suggests a wide variety of ways to use social media to supplement training, but many of these opportunities also exist for formal education and are mobile accessible. Particularly for mobile use, a representative sample includes capturing videos or photos of relevant locations or having a tweetstream to accompany a presentation.

META-LEARNING

Interacting with others requires a suite of skills, and doing so through technology adds another set. The ubiquity possible with mobility provides some additional considerations for communication, listening, participation, and more.

Mobile communications often feature *textese*, which is texts using shorthand such as gr8 for great and acronyms like LOL for laugh out loud (i.e., funny). Driven by character limitations and the difficulty of using mobile keyboards, such language can be expected to surface in mobile tools as well. This may not be a problem, but reflection on appropriate communication style for the context deserves explicit discussion.

A different problem may exist when communication tools are ubiquitous. What constitutes listening, if multiple channels are being used? Does looking at a tweetstream while someone is talking help or hinder processing? These questions are worth having a conversation about.

Similarly, the question arises of what can be considered as participation. Does contributing in class mean talking, tweeting, or sharing mind maps? What are the expectations? On principle, legitimate participation ought to include the ability to ask questions and to offer opinions. What channels are to be considered as appropriate and how such contributions are evaluated will make differences.

Mobile etiquette may also be different. Certainly, whether a cell phone is turned off or not increasingly signals the importance of a communication. Does a lecture count? If the mobile device is off, it may not be able to participate via microblogs (e.g., Twitter), yet while you might not want a phone ringing in class, you might want learners to be able to chat. You will need to reconcile the trade-offs to determine what's feasible. Working with the students provides an opportunity to talk about etiquette more broadly, particularly compromises and what it means for learning.

For each of these issues, policies can be set for the classroom, but a discussion of what was considered and how a decision was made can lead to the broader discussion of what learning means in a mobile era and how the parameters may change in different contexts. What constitutes institutional policy versus a particular instructor's may also be worthy of explicit consideration.

SUMMARY

The benefits of social learning are more powerful processing. Mobile devices offer the ability to interact more flexibly, wherever and whenever a learner has inspiration. Learners can communicate and collaborate whenever the thought strikes.

Students can share thoughts, respond to others, and work together, all of which have useful outcomes for learning. Inherent to mobile learning, however, is the ability to do things unique to a location or time, whether capturing and sharing personal experience or working together. Further opportunities come with the ability to plan activities that require cooperation or collaboration in a particular context, the topic of the next chapter.

PRACTICE

1. What social media capabilities are available in your existing learning infrastructure? What are the mobile access mechanisms for those capabilities?

2. How can you use mobile tools to get learner participation in class? What would they do? How would it be incorporated?

3. What are some locations it would make sense for learners to visit collectively? What could they do, and what would the learning outcomes be? What are the mobile tools they would use to accomplish these tasks?

CHANNEL CHECKLIST

Consider this list as a prod to considering alternative mechanisms:

- Voice
- Chat
- Microblog
- Blog
- Wiki
- Media sharing (images, audio, video, links)

Going Beyond

A few approaches constitute the cutting edge of mobile applications by combining some of the Four C's and pushing beyond the obvious categories already covered. These include the A* realities: augmented reality and alternate reality, and adaptive delivery.

I have taken a straightforward view of context to date, and I want to push it a bit further. So far, we have largely talked about context in a static sense, where information is stored in a location, associated with a task, or requested by a learner. However, an additional step is to dynamically look at the location a learner is in and push information that is of interest to that particular learner. This requires a slightly more sophisticated architecture to deliver content according to some rules, not just having it available in the world or on the device.

AUGMENTED REALITY

Here we are talking about having a model of learners—at least what course they are doing—and a model of the information available, and then tracking learners' location and using a set of rules to provide custom information opportunistically. This is the essence of augmented reality, and a prototypical example is a car global positioning system (GPS). In this model, the system knows a person's goal and current situation and introduces some extra information into the environment such as an appropriately oriented map and voice directions.

The ultimate example is the type of capabilities provided by companies like Layar that use GPS location, take in directional information from the device compass, and then layer information onto the image from the camera onto the screen so you can "see" what is around you. If you're interested in food, for example, you hold up your mobile device and scan around you, and the picture on your screen from your camera has pointers to what restaurants are available.

The Museum of London has an augmented reality educational application that, based on a person's location, overlays pictures of that location from the past (Museum of London, 2010). The ability to compare the current look with the past provides a contrast that helps contextualize the changes that history and technology bring.

An alternative version of this model that is still underexploited is augmenting *when*. For example, a system knows that an individual has a task such as a meeting and a learning goal such as running better meetings. The system could then provide some preparatory content beforehand, a job aid during, and a self-evaluation rubric afterward (or connect the person to a mentor). This enables a learner's life to become a learning opportunity instead of the learning creating artificial situations. Such systems are not yet in use, but the potential is there as an ideal to work toward (Quinn, 2004).

So, if a learning goal was negotiation and if the learner faced a real negotiation situation as part of an internship, preparatory material could be provided before such a situation. A brief summary of the principles of negotiation could be sent to the learner's mobile device before the meeting begins; negotiation support could be provided via your device during the negotiation, such as a checklist; and afterward an advisor could be prompted to call the learner to ask questions about how the principles of negotiation were displayed (or not) during the actual event.

The underlying concept is to look at tasks that learners are assigned or decisions they have to make that reflect the current learning concepts and to leverage any real-world occurrences to enable them to serve as extensions of the learning situation. We mimic real-world practice in the learning environment, but if there is real-world practice, or the ability to more closely couple the learning context to the performance context, the transfer distance is minimized.

Interestingly, the distinction between virtual worlds (e.g., Second Life and equivalents) and mobile augmented reality begin to blur. While people can't fly in the real world, they can have artificial objects inhabiting a space via mobile tools. Learners could cocreate additional representations as well, providing commentary and new conceptualizations to specific locations. The powerful social three-dimensional (3-D) capabilities of virtual worlds may at least partially be ported to the real world via mobile technologies.

Another possibility is the broader picture of location-specific information. Jim Spohrer (1998), then at Apple, proposed WorldBoard, a mechanism to add information to places, augmenting reality. Mobile tools provide a mechanism to allow such information to create valuable learning opportunities, both via information at a location (preferably customized to the learner's interests) and via learner additions to that information Such capabilities are now being delivered via Layar, a browser and platform that allows others to make location-specific information available to mobile devices.

ALTERNATE REALITY

There are reasons to create artificial experiences that are mobile delivered, not just augmented information. Here, we are talking alternate reality, where a situation is presented that isn't real but appears to be so. This is not unique to mobile, but there are specific learning objectives where mobile adds unique value. The ability for both location and time independence is one, and location specificity is a second.

A prototypical example would be emergency training exercises, where a simulated catastrophe requires trained response. Emergency crews use mobile devices to communicate as needed, and consequently a training simulation has a closer degree of fidelity to the real event in this way, which maximizes transfer. Whether external manifestations of the effects are represented, the learning activity is real. Such activities can be human controlled or built with an engine that drives the simulation.

The University of Aberdeen has a flood simulation that is conducted by simple messaging system (SMS). In this simulation, communications come in concerning a flood. The flood isn't real, but the messages play out in a time frame like one would happen, and the learner is asked to make the decisions that an appropriate administrator would be required to make. It is an alternate reality scenario that plays out over time using text messages. And disaster crews do use mobile tools to coordinate.

On the principle that simulations can be turned into games, the extreme examples of this are the alternate reality games, such as the ones run to promote the movie *AI* (*The Beast*) and the game *Halo* (*I Love Bees*). In each, media cues led learners to start tracking down clues that supported a background story. While not specifically mobile, they did require real-time responses (such as a phone ringing at a particular street corner at a particular time and someone needing to answer it).

By creating a separate storyline and embedding decisions that require applying the concepts in a time-sensitive manner, you are creating dynamic learning experiences. With Red7 (2011), we created a demo of a sales-training alternate reality game a number of years ago that also captures the opportunity. In this game, learners had to choose which potential customer to contact, such as by e-mail, and then the customer would get back to them, perhaps leaving a voicemail. The game played out across several days, as the individual the learner contacted might take a day to respond. Over time, learners interact with the potential customer, establishing the relationship and gathering information to the point that a sale could be made. This is not mobile specific, but it could include text messages or other communication channels (e.g., Twitter, Skype) and uses the device the learner has. Such an alternate reality game—in which learners role-play—embeds decisions based upon knowledge and skills in a compelling way. Meaningful practice that drives learners to relevant knowledge in engaging ways creates an engaging experience that other mechanisms cannot match.

A related approach would be to use the framework of role-playing games to let learners take on personas with goals and play out those roles, with reflection afterward to viscerally experience issues. As mentioned in a previous chapter, *Online Role-Playing Games* (Wills, Leigh, & Ip, 2011) provides a great exposition and guidance in the use of this approach, where conflicting goals provide insight into issues historical or current. Extending this to mobile may again more closely mimic the way such actions would play out in the real world and also would provide an immediacy that heightens engagement. Players could mimic the revolutions in the Middle East in 2011 and could play, for example, resistance leaders, existing governments, neighboring countries, major world powers, and the United Nations and use social media to communicate using something like an updated and mobile version of the work of Vincent and Shepherd (1998). Again, this isn't unique to mobile, but the ability for new events to be tracked whenever and wherever could add immediacy to events. Similarly, the introduction of information into a scenario during play could be handled by mobile devices in realistic ways.

Location-specific actions can also be developed, including local events historical or fictitious, catastrophic or man-made. Taking an example like the University of Abderdeen's SMS flood simulation and making it multiplayer and location specific would be one opportunity. Giving learners roles like local authorities from different agencies and having them gather information from particular locations and coordinate the data could illustrate a variety of issues in administration, safety, and more. The goal is to map learning decisions into real-world situations and simulate them.

There is a further extension to this thought. We can have systems that play out activity dynamically, looking at both the location and the context of what already has happened. Thus, we can have alternate reality games that combine augmented and alternate reality games, adding in reality augmentation that supplements the alternate reality experience.

ADAPTIVE DELIVERY

The received wisdom, as shown in Figure 8.1, is that the web has moved from 1.0 to 2.0, from producer-generated content to user-generated content (among other interpretations of web 2.0). Looking forward, we see web 3.0, *system-generated content*. Here, systems that have access to rich models of the learner and the content can use rules to combine content *on the fly* to customize the learning experience. We already see this in customized experiences such as movie and product recommendations on shopping sites. The ideal is personalized performance support and learning.

The necessary component to successfully deliver against this dream is to ensure that content is sufficiently granular and appropriately (and richly) tagged as to its properties, as discussed in Chapter Five. A principled basis for granularity is the smallest role a piece of content can play in a learning role. (And a pragmatic one would be the smallest chunk of content you'd give to one learner versus another in an individually mentored context.) The benefits of such efforts are first for instructor-defined and learner-selected delivery, but we can go further.

With rich models of the learner, the content, the context, and the learner's goals, the delivery of content can be customized appropriately (see Figure 8.2).

Figure 8.1 Web Generations.

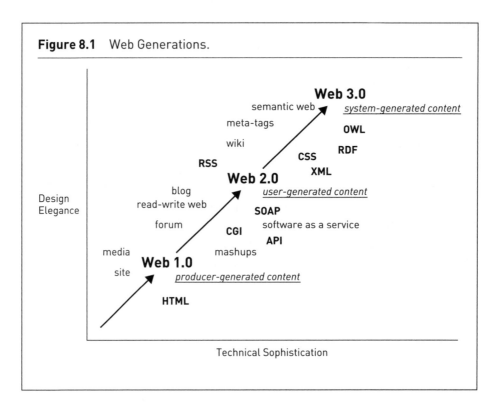

One basis for such prescriptive delivery includes writing rules that encapsulate the results of research and theory and mapping best principles into recommendations. A second basis is to mine data from learning analytics, data captured across the usage of learning systems. Ultimately, what could be optimal would be to create the best rules and then let machine learning from the data refine the rules (an approach we were implementing back around 2000 with the Intellectricity™ system).

This differs from the Intelligent Tutoring System (ITS) approach. ITSs create deep models of performance, evaluate learner performance in comparison, and then intervene in theory-specific ways. On the other hand, this approach would look for research-based or emergent differences in learner behavior in learning, and adapt on that basis. So, instead of noticing that a subtraction process was wrong, such a system would look at whether there are repeated difficulties with graphs versus charts or tables, for example.

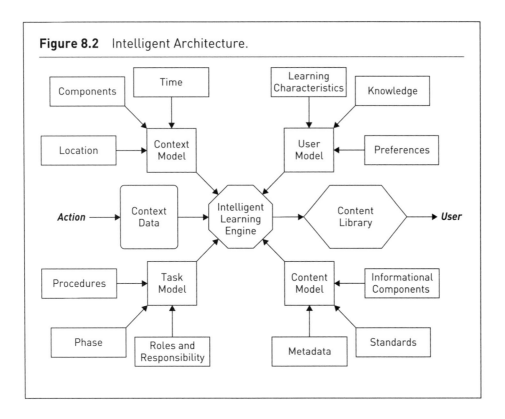

Figure 8.2 Intelligent Architecture.

The goal would be create a personalized learning experience that would provide content, practice, examples, and more in a sequence that depends on the learner, the learner's recent and overall performance, and the learning goals. More optimally, it would also recognize a learner's current context and would take advantage of devices or location-specific information. Thus, a person visiting a city might be recommended to visit a relevant museum and have customized content that addresses his particular learning needs. A finer granularity can be imagined as well.

MOVING FORWARD

The ultimate goal is to find the optimal learning experience for the audience, taking into account their context, learning goals, preferences, and more and using all available channels. In the longer term, we may approach what I call *slow learning*, moving our learning models from events to microinterventions. We know from Chapter Three that massed practice doesn't work, yet for a variety of pragmatic reasons we have been required to make modular learning experiences.

Consider, instead, taking a long-term relationship with the learner and doing a more continuous development. The metaphor is watering plants: The current model represents flooding, where much of the water evaporates before it does any good, whereas the alternative is drip irrigation, with more appropriately placed and sized application of water. Mobile technologies give us the tools to start distributing learning in space and time, and we should be taking advantage of it. Think about reactivating, reconceptualizing, recontextualizing, and reapplying knowledge more often in smaller chunks as a way to start thinking in about the possibilities for mobile learning to transform higher education. We have the tools to do so, and now we must consider the interim steps to take and what an associated design process would look like. If we can make the academy more effective, we have a moral imperative to do so. If we can make it more efficient without comprising effectiveness, we have a financial incentive to do so. If we can improve outcomes overall, it is an opportunity we should not pass up.

PRACTICE

1. Think about what a completely mobile-delivered higher education experience would be like. What would the learner see, hear, and *do*?

2. Consider what you would do if you had magic: What would you do to create the optimal learning experience if you had no technological limits? You may be surprised to find out that you can come closer than you think and that more is possible than you imagined.

Getting Going: Organizational Issues

All of the options detailed to this point do not exist in a vacuum but depend on the organizational context and have implications for the organizational context as well. Issues of development and deployment come into play, as does management and policy. This is different from providing the administrative services discussed in Chapter Four but instead take the administrative perspective on implementation, management, and policy. Much is traditional (e.g., design principles, development concerns) but is worth revisiting, and the unique aspects of mobile also are highlighted.

As a first step, we need to return to the environmental scan of Chapter Four. We need to consider the infrastructure available, such as platforms and tools, resources such as faculty and design and development teams, and policies on things such as information technology (IT) and student support. Note that the environment for development is incredibly dynamic and consequently is too hard to provide inclusive prescriptions here, but we can review some alternatives and the trade-offs.

DESIGN

The first issue is to review mobile-specific design principles. The unique characteristics of mobile devices put a focus on simplicity and elegance.

One of the sources of principles for mobile design is John Carroll's minimalism (see Carroll, 1990). Applying his principles to a word processor, he created 25 cards that were more effective than the instructionally designed manual. The principles used included giving credit to the learner for preexisting knowledge, focusing on the learner's goals, and looking for the least support necessary—what I call the *least assistance principle*, as in, "What's the least I can do for you?" (Quinn, 2011).

These principles are echoed in the Zen of Palm (2003). These were a set of design guidelines that captured the essence of what led to the success of the Palm Pilot. The principles relevant here are: don't try to do everything and instead focus on the top 80% of what users do; reduce the number of steps required; and include users in the design process.

That latter step is worth reiterating. Good design benefits from user involvement, to the extent that it has its own label: *participatory design*. Particularly with mobile devices, users will have experience and expectations that will be important for the ultimate user experience.

The general usability goals very much apply here: Minimize steps to accomplish a task, minimize errors, support learnability and relearnability, and ensure the highest user satisfaction. You should be creating metrics in the design process that will be the basis of testing and determine when the goals are achieved. These include usability and learning goals. Games will have the addition of engagement metrics. Good principles for interface design such as leveraging existing user knowledge by maintaining consistency with other interfaces, platform standards, and internal navigation.

DEVELOPMENT

Somehow, we need to create content, interactions, and support for hosting of both what we develop and what comes from the learners, be it data capture or conversations. Depending on the institutional context, there are a variety of options. If tools are built into the infrastructure or if existing tools have mobile output, it is possible that learning designers, faculty or staff, may be able to produce their own resources with minimal changes.

Typically, institutions range along a continuum from the instructor having control to a situation where a team designs the course for various instructors to deliver. In between, there are situations where faculty can get help to institutions where every course gets support. The driver of the locus of control for learning quality can be the perceived status or the commercial basis of the institution. However, learning design ownership, ranging from a faculty member to team development, may have emerged historically but should be considered consciously.

Naturally, there are trade-offs in the alternatives. Individual knowledge and freedom are manifest in situations where the control for the learning experience is devolved to the individual instructor. Risks with that approach include faculty who may be experts in their field but perhaps not on pedagogy. On the other hand, institutional control supports a consistent experience, but perhaps at the cost of mediocrity and lack of inspiration. In between are opportunities to combine the two. This is as true of mobile as it is in anything else.

To achieve the outcomes outlined in Chapter Three for quality learning, both pedagogical competence and technological competence are necessary. Similarly, taking a strategic perspective is also necessary. Consequently, support for mobile learning is likely to be needed.

Strategically

The tools available are in constant flux, so no recommendations can be easily made. The primary recommendation is to build the mobile option into the content development processes. There are really two options: (1) platform based, where the learning management system (LMS) has content development and mobile delivery options; or (2) tool based, where you use a suite of tools to develop content independent of the delivery platform and the content products may be deliverable to mobile devices separately or through the learning platform. The easy way to start is to find out if the existing tools or platform support mobile delivery; they may be built in. Similarly, media conversion is also likely built in, and, if not, tools are available for free. Web access is also a potential path.

Having individuals (e.g., instructors) create and load their own content using an LMS that has built-in mobile hosting is one approach. As mentioned in Chapter Four, Blackboard has a mobile option, and other LMSs either do or will soon. Some tools are also specifically designed to allow content to be entered and delivered via mobile devices.

Publicly available apps may meet specific needs for learners or support development. From presentation applications to various lab tools, apps continue to appear that are designed to meet specific needs. Furthermore, some capabilities may be developed for free (e.g., the Layar augmented reality platform) using free tools.

The other approach to mobile development is typically driven by instructional developers supporting academics, either alone or as a team. Such developers often use myriad tools, depending on whether they are developing video, audio, documents, animations, interactives, and more. These tools increasingly have the capabilities to deliver a variety of output file formats. Alternatively, a wide variety of content conversion tools are available as well at low or no cost. Rather than produce all of the possible file formats, an organization should choose a mobile format for each file type that will be supported. Then, workflows should be expanded to systematically generate mobile as a standard component of the output.

Custom development of mobile-specific applications will likely currently still have to be custom or outsourced for now, but, again, even interactive tools have or will soon have mobile format outputs. Also, packages exist for particular options; for instance, simple messaging system (SMS) tools are available, as are voice.

Deployment is a second issue. One option is to have a way to preload or deliver mobile solutions onto devices proactively. This is hard, however, unless the institution is providing the hardware. If the institution is providing the devices, control over what appears on the devices is not a problem. Otherwise, it may need to be discretionary, in that a subset of all possible devices is agreed to be supported, but there are no requirements for mobile access to be able to pass a class. In the case of learner-provided devices, the options include institution-provided portals or the potential use of other resources.

IMPLEMENTATION

Just as with any intervention, do not assume that all the pieces will be in place to successfully execute. Initiating a new project requires the basic elements of organizational change. As Cross and Dublin (2002) pointed out, elements such as a vision, stakeholder buy-in, and messaging are necessary.

All e-learning strategy requires a vision of the larger performance ecosystem (Quinn, 2009a), in which the overall picture of e-learning, performance support, content models (greater integration), mobile (broader distribution), social learning, and more are considered (See Figure 9.1). At the end, the goal is to have a coherent environment, in this case for learning. That is, a solution is desired that blends the technologies to match the right learning outcome to the right delivery medium.

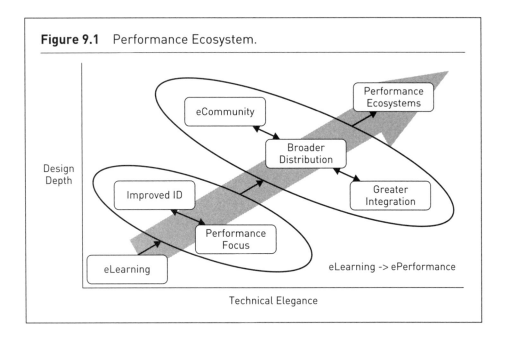

Figure 9.1 Performance Ecosystem.

To do that effectively, you need to have a vision of where you want to go, and then pick your projects that take you in a systematic way from where you are to the desired end state. The aim is to pick projects that build an infrastructure in a way that contributes to the overall picture rather than to idiosyncratic projects requiring effort that is not scalable and that detract from the overall focus.

On the other hand, initial pilots are to be encouraged, as learning from these projects contributes to the understanding applied to the larger goal. These two views are not incommensurate: If the resources taken for the pilot leverage as much existing infrastructure as possible, the extra overhead is small and factored into the overall plan, and the lessons learned by those involved get applied going forward.

From a learner perspective, how do mobile devices complement the desktop or classroom activities to create a full learning experience? That is the real question to be answered. The concept of learning experience design holds here, but in a broader sense. You may be just developing one solution, but the learner will perceive it as part of the whole learning ecosystem provided by the institution.

Evaluating the solution is similarly important. Metrics were discussed earlier, but they will ultimately need to be collected and evaluated. Triangulation is useful as well, combining quantitative data on learning outcomes and usage with subjective evaluation of learner experience.

POLICIES

Overall, there is the issue of institutional policy on mobile delivery. Policy areas include accessibility, appropriate behavior, support scope and mechanisms, security, and privacy.

The short answer to many of these issues is that the problem is already addressed in another channel and the lessons apply. This is true for social media, for instance. Institutions should already have policies about what constitutes appropriate messages and behavior that won't be tolerated (e.g., cyberbullying). Thus, a separate policy isn't necessary.

Similarly, support policies are likely already in place but will need to be evaluated in light of any changes due to mobile initiatives. And the use of devices will already have principles (e.g., mobile phones need to be on silent in class; e-mail will be responded to within 48 hours as a quality of service issue), but again policies will need to be reviewed.

Two other areas for the ethics of IT use are also already covered. There is an ethical requirement to let learners know what information is being kept about them, but that's true regardless of the technology. When any assessment is being made at a distance, it is also incumbent on learners to take responsibility for their own work if such freedom is provided. This is true across distance learning and is not unique to mobile, though as mentioned earlier video cameras in devices may make proctoring possible.

A related issue is security. One issue is security of transmissions. Any individual information about students needs to be carefully protected. In general, commercial education solutions have this covered, and internal IT departments are well aware of the issues. The only concern would be free web sites and third-party tools. Ideally such tools and sites won't require personal data, but as a consequence that is an issue that should be required to be investigated for any mobile offering chosen. Consequently, any tools like Facebook and Twitter that require users to provide details may not be able to be required as assignments, or alternate mechanisms need to exist.

Accessibility for disabilities should also already be addressed. Whatever policies are in place for the web likely will at least partly serve. As the World Wide Web Consortium's (2008) Web Accessibility Initiative says, "Users of mobile devices and people with disabilities experience similar barriers when interacting with Web content."

The policy requirements are likely also already in existence for support, as IT already supports two major laptop and desktop operating systems, and the web. The greater variety of mobile platforms, however, makes it difficult to be equitable. Alternatively, the responsibility can be left up to the vendor of the solution, with the compromise of higher licensing fees and potential barriers to complete equity in access in the vendor scope of solution.

Security is another issue that breaks up into separate concerns. Mobile devices can be lost, and any data on the device might be compromised. This argues for web delivery of information rather than storing locally on the device and no persistent downloads for any sensitive information such as user data. A second security issue is transmission of information securely. While solutions exist, regular IT security in data transmission is typically sufficient.

A top issue is whether to support learner-owned devices or to provide them. All development and assistance issues center on the scope of devices supported. The benefits of institution-specified (and subsidized) devices are the ability to limit resources to specific platforms. The downside is initial cost and that as technologies change, particularly in the case of mobile devices, obsolescence is an ongoing problem. If you choose to use the learner's devices, you either have to have a multiplicity of solutions, or risk missing some of the potential audience. This will change as interoperability and standards develop, but the current environment is not mature enough.

Some institutions have provided devices—for example, Duke University's experiment with providing iPods and Abilene Christian University's providing either an iPod Touch or iPhone (in the latter case, the student was required to fund the phone service to minimize institutional financial liability). Seton Hall has announced that all incoming students will get iPads, which not only facilitates mobile uses but also serves as a marketing tool. The benefits are a common platform to develop for, which provides better leverage of resources at the cost of providing support. The enthusiasm for such devices may also intrigue potential students.

The results have been mixed. Duke ended their iPod experiment after two years, while Abilene Christian University has continued to build upon their initial investment. Stanford had mixed results with introducing iPads into the medical school curriculum. Issues include the difficulty in providing wireless access across campus and the relative value learners find in the mobile solutions (Keller, 2011).

A final issue is governance, oversight, and ownership of the mobile strategy. Ideally, participation is representative of the institution's constituencies. Whether governance should be separate for mobile from other IT and e-learning is an institutional decision, though mobile learning, like e-learning, probably *should* be jointly owned by IT and the unit responsible for student learning. Other mobile services, such as those concerning administrative needs, may be more appropriately owned purely by IT. The need for governance, however, is clear.

Governance is about oversight of management decisions surrounding investments. If indications are any guide, mobile will be an increasing component of IT strategy, and consequently mobile cannot be considered a minor activity, though perhaps it will end up being merely a delivery channel for more comprehensive services. The concerns for mobile indicated above, however, suggest that scrutiny from the perspective of accountability will be important.

Governance includes the content, the hardware, and the resources applied. Concerns will include policy, security, support, and content life cycle. Staffing and development processes will also be an issue. The concerns are not only security, but effectiveness and efficiency as well. Ensuring oversight provides the opportunities to link the organization's strategic goals with mobile implementation.

YOU GOTTA BE *IN* IT TO *GET* IT

At this point, I hope you have gotten excited about the possibilities and have begun to lay out your plans to bring mobile into the repertoire of learning solutions you use to create the best learning experience for your students.

To really grasp the potential of mobile learning, just as with social media, you have to *use* it to really understand.

First, you need to push your own use of mobile devices to see how far they can assist you in learning more opportunistically and performing more comprehensively. Be proactive in thinking how you might use your device to make yourself more capable. What content can you load or access? What computations might it assist with? What can you capture, whether audio, photo, or video? And who might you reach out to? Also, experiment with different devices: Get thee to an electronics store and try out at least the handheld gaming platforms, a different smartphone from the one you have, and a tablet.

Talk to other people. How are they using mobile devices? Surprising examples include taking pictures of hotel room numbers, parking garage locations, and bus schedules. If you inquire, you will find a wealth of examples your friends and colleagues are using. These models provide rich inspiration for new ideas.

In particular, talk to students. What do they do? What do they want? What do they think would be a good idea?

Look for examples: Where are you seeing mobile learning and performance happening? What are you hearing at conferences, reading on the web, being told by vendors, and seeing from students?

And, of course, look for opportunities. Where do practitioners perform? Where could learners perform? What contexts could they visit? Which ones do they already go to?

There is one caveat, however. With the current enthusiasm for mobile, it might seem expedient to consider a mobile initiative for marketing purposes. However, after awareness increases, if the initiative does not deliver real learning value the venality of the move will undermine the effort. Focus on delivering real learning value; the opportunity *is* there, and so too should the focus be.

Enhancing the learner experience is key. The administrative possibilities are valuable, but the ability to improve learning outcomes is the ultimate goal. By distributing and augmenting the learning experience across space and time, the opportunity exists to create learning that is retained longer and transferred more appropriately. More, mobile has the potential to be more transformative than even e-learning was. With a more distributed learning experience, we can start rethinking the underlying models and perhaps get closer to the individual mentorship that characterizes the ideal.

Overall, at this point there is little else to do but to tell you to get on with it. Mobilize your resources and your learning.

PRACTICE

1. What is your existing development process, and how can you systematically integrate mobile into it? What content development processes do you have? What are your delivery channels?

2. What mobile-relevant policies currently exist in your institution that you can appropriate? What new policies do you think you need to have?

3. What are the trade-offs for your institution to select and perhaps subsidize a device or suite thereof versus working toward a learner-owned device solution?

Bibliography

Abilene Christian University. (2011). Solutions for the 21st-century university.
   http://www.acu.edu/technology/mobilelearning/vision/solutions/index.html

Ausubel, D. P. (1978). The use of advance organizers in the learning and retention of meaningful verbal material. *Journal of Educational Psychology*, *51*(5), 267–272.

Barrows, H. S. (1986). A taxonomy of problem-based learning methods. *Medical Education*, *20*(6), 481–486.

Blackboard. (2011). Support: FAQs and getting started.
   http://www.blackboard.com/Mobile/Resources/FAQ.aspx

Bloom, B. S. (1956). *Cognitive domain, taxonomy of educational objectives— The classification of educational goals.* New York: David McKay Company.

Bozarth, J. (2010). *Social media for trainers.* San Francisco: Pfeiffer.

Bruner, J. S. (1961). The act of discovery. *Harvard Educational Review*, *31*(1), 21–32.

Campus Computing. (2010). The 2010 Campus Computing Survey.
   http://www.campuscomputing.net/sites/www.campuscomputing.net/files/Green-CampusComputing2010.pdf

Carroll, J. M. (1990). *The Nurnberg Funnel: Designing minimalist instruction for practical computer skill.* Cambridge, MA: MIT Press.

Carter, D. (2009). Cellphones used to deliver course content. eSchool News.
   http://www.eschoolnews.com/2009/07/06/cell-phones-used-to-deliver-course-content/

Clark, R. C., & Mayer, R. E. (2003). *e-learning and the science of instruction.* San Francisco: Pfeiffer.

Clarke, A. C. (1984). *Profiles of the future: An inquiry into the limits of the possible* (revised ed.). New York: Henry Holt & Co.

CNET. (2011). Oklahoma State students, faculty tout iPad in classroom. http://news.cnet.com/8301-13506_3-20059325-17.html

Cognition and Technology Group at Vanderbilt. (1990). Anchored instruction and its relationship to situated cognition. *Educational Researcher*, *19*(6), 2–10.

Collins, A., Brown, J. S., & Holum, A. (1991). Cognitive apprenticeship: Making thinking visible. *American Educator*, *15*(3), 6–11, 38–46.

Cross, J., & Dublin, L. (2002). *Implementing e-learning*. Alexandria, VA: ASTD.

Dick, W., Carey, L., & Carey, D. O. (2004). *The systematic design of instruction* (6th ed.). Boston: Allyn & Bacon.

Gery, G. (1995). *Electronic performance support systems: How and why to remake the workplace through the strategic application of technology*. Toland, MA: Gery Performance Press.

Gick, M. L., & Holyoak, K. J. (1980). Analogical problem solving. *Cognitive Psychology*, *12*, 306–355.

Gick, M. L., & Holyoak, K. J. (1983). Schema induction and analogical transfer. *Cognitive Psychology*, *15*, 1–38.

Google. (2010). Barcelona: Mobile first. http://googlemobile.blogspot.com/2010/02/barcelona-mobile-first.html

Jalali, A., Trottier, D., Tremblay, M., & Hincke, M. (2011). Administering a gross anatomy exam using mobile technology. eLearn Mag. http://www.elearnmag.org/subpage.cfm?section=articles&article=152-1

International Telecommunications Union (ITU). (2010). The world in 2010: ICT facts and figures. http://www.itu.int/ITU-D/ict/material/FactsFigures2010.pdf

Keller, J. (1983). Motivational design of instruction. In C. Reigeluth (Ed.), *Instructional-design theories and models: An overview of their current status*. Mahwah, NJ: Lawrence Erlbaum.

Keller, J. (2011). The slow-motion mobile campus. *The Chronicle of Higher Education*. http://chronicle.com/article/The-Slow-Motion-Mobile-Campus/127380/

Kukulska-Hulme, A., and Traxler, J. (Eds.). (2005). *Mobile learning: A handbook for educators and trainers*. London: Routledge.

Larkin, J. H., & Simon, H. A. (1987). Why a diagram is (sometimes) worth ten thousand words. *Cognitive Science*, *11*, 65–99.

Laurillard, D. (1993). *Rethinking university teaching: A framework for effective use of educational technology*. London: Routledge.

Long, P. D., & Holeton, R. (2009). Signposts of the revolution? What we talk about when we talk about learning spaces. *Educause Review*, *44* (2). http://www.educause.edu/EDUCAUSE+Review/EDUCAUSEReviewMagazine Volume44/SignpostsoftheRevolutionWhatWe/163798

Mager, R. (1975). *Preparing instructional objectives* (2d ed.). Belmont, CA: Lake Publishing Co.

Metcalf, D. S. (2006). *mLearning: Mobile learning and performance in the palm of your hand*. Amherst, MA: HRD Press.

Mobile Oxford. (2011). Features. http://m.ox.ac.uk/desktop/#features

Mtld.mobi. (2011). dotMobi. http://mtld.mobi

Museum of London. (2010). Streetmuseum. http://www.museumoflondon.org.uk/Resources/app/you-are-here-app/index.html

Nielsen. (2010). Smartphones to overtake feature phones in U.S. by 2011. http://blog.nielsen.com/nielsenwire/consumer/smartphones-to-overtake-feature-phones-in-u-s-by-2011/

Nielsen, J. (2011). Mobile content is twice as difficult. http://www.useit.com/alertbox/mobile-content-comprehension.html

Open Education. (2008). Student shortcomings—Anything but masters of technology. http://www.openeducation.net/2008/01/19/student-shortcomings-anything-but-masters-of-technology/

OnDevice. (2011). The mobile only Internet generation. http://www.slideshare.net/OnDevice/the-mobile-only-internet-generation

Pew. (2010). Social media and young adults. http://www.pewinternet.org/Reports/2010/Social-Media-and-Young-Adults/Part-2/1-Cell-phones.aspx

Palm. (2003). The path to enlightenment. http://www.accessdevnet.com/docs/zenofpalm/Enlightenment.html

Parry, D. (2011). Mobile perspectives: On teaching mobile literacy. *Educause Review*, *46*(2). http://www.elearnmag.org/subpage.cfm?section=articles&article=152-1

Quinn, C. N. (2000). Learning objects and instruction components. *Educational Technology & Society*, *3*(2). http://ifets.ieee.org/periodical/vol_2_2000/discuss_summary_0200.html

Quinn, C. N. (2004). Learning at large: Situating learning in the bigger picture of action in the world. *Educational Technology Magazine*, *44*(4). Englewood Cliffs, NJ: Educational Technology Publications.

Quinn, C. N. (2005). *Engaging learning: Designing e-learning simulation games*. San Francisco: Pfeiffer.

Quinn, C. N. (2009a). Populating the LearnScape: e-learning as strategy. In M. Allen (Ed.), *Michael Allen's e-learning annual 2009*. Pfeiffer: San Francisco.

Quinn, C. N. (2009b). Social networking: Bridging formal and informal learning. *Learning Solutions Magazine*. http://www.learningsolutionsmag.com/articles/57/social-networking-bridging-formal-and-informal-learning

Quinn, C. N. (2009c). The 7 C's of natural learning. http://blog.learnlets.com/?p=1203

Quinn, C. N. (2011). *Designing mLearning: Tapping into the mobile revolution for organizational performance*. San Francisco: Pfeiffer.

Quinn, C. N., Mehan, H., Levin, J. A., & Black, S. D. (1983). Real education in non-real time: The use of electronic message systems for instruction. *Instructional Science, 11,* 313–327.

Red 7. (2011). Red 7 mixed reality technologies. http://web.red7.com/fits.html

Reigeluth, C., & Stein, F. (1983). The elaboration theory of instruction. In C. Reigeluth (Ed.), *Instructional design theories and models.* Hillsdale, NJ: Erlbaum Associates.

Rossett, A., & Shafer, L. (2006). *Job aids and performance support: Moving from knowledge in the classroom to knowledge everywhere.* Pfeiffer: San Francisco.

Schlenker, B. (2009). E-learning 2.0: The 'E' is for everybody. The eLearning guild online forum: E-learning 2.0 and beyond-Practical real-world solutions using new technology approaches. http://www.elearningguild.com/showFile.cfm?id=3393

Schoenfeld, A. H. (1992). Learning to think mathematically: Problem-solving, metacognition, and sense-making in mathematics. In D. Grouws (Ed.), *Handbook for research on mathematics teaching and learning.* New York: MacMillan.

Soloway, E., Grant, W., Tinker, R., Roschelle, J., Mills, M., Resnick, M., Berg, R., & Eisenberg, M. (1999). Science in the palms of their hands. *Communications of the Association for Computing Machinery, 42,* 8.

Spiro, R. J., Feltovich, P. J., Jacobsen, M. J., & Coulson, R. L. (1992). Cognitive flexibility, constructivism and hypertext: Random access instruction for advanced knowledge acquisition in ill-structured domains. In T. Duffy & D. Jonassen (Eds.), *Constructivism and the technology of instruction.* Hillsdale, NJ: Erlbaum.

Spohrer, J. (1998). Worldboard. http://www.worldboard.org/pub/spohrer/wbconcept/default.html

Stanford University. (2011). Stanford University: Mobile. http://mobile.stanford.edu/

Sugrue, B. (2002). Problems with Bloom's taxonomy. http://www.performancexpress.org/0212/mainframe0212.html#title3

SunGard. (2010). SunGard higher education previews extensible mobile framework. http://www.sungardhe.com/news.aspx?id=1677

Thalheimer, W. (2006). Spacing learning over time. http://willthalheimer.typepad.com/files/spacing_learning_over_time_2006.pdf

The Street. (2011). Tablet sales to eat into PC market: Report. http://www.thestreet.com/story/11045534/1/tablet-sales-to-eat-into-pc-market-report.html

TUAW. (2011). Enterprise iPad adoption up to 80 percent in Fortune 100. http://www.tuaw.com/2011/02/14/enterprise-ipad-adoption-up-to-80-percent-in-fortune-100/

VanLehn, K. (1990). *Mind bugs: Origins of procedural misconception.* Cambridge, MA: MIT Press.

Van Merriënboer, J.J.G. (1997). *Training complex cognitive skills: A four-component instructional design model for technical training.* Englewood Cliffs, NJ: Educational Technology Publications.

Vincent, A., & Shepherd, J. (1998). Experiences in teaching Middle East politics via internet-based role-play simulations. *Journal of Interactive Media in Education, 98*(11). http://jime.open.ac.uk/article/1998-11/40

Vygotsky, L. S. (1978). *Mind in society* (M. Cole, V. John-Steiner, S. Scribner, & E. Souberman, Eds.). Cambridge, MA: Harvard University Press.

Wexler, S., Schlenker, B., Brown, J., Metcalf, D., Quinn, C., Thor, E., Van Barneveld, A., & Wagner, E. (2007). *360 research report mobile learning: What it is, why it matters, and how to incorporate it into your learning strategy.* Santa Rosa CA: eLearning Guild.

Whitehead, A. N. (1929). *The aims of education and other essays.* New York: Free Press.

Wills, S., Leigh, E., & Ip, A. (2011). *The power of role-based e-learning.* New York: Routledge.

Woodill, G. (2010). *The mobile learning edge: Tools and technologies for developing your teams.* New York: McGraw-Hill.

World Wide Web Consortium. (2008). Web content accessibility and mobile web: Making a web site accessible both for people with disabilities and for mobile devices. http://www.w3.org/WAI/mobile/

Index

B

Barnes & Noble Nook, 59
Barrows, H. S., 25, 34
Beever, G., 52, 60
Behavior, learner: adaptive delivery and, 92; guidelines for, 79; policies related to, 100
Berg, R., 3
Biking rules, 43
Black, S. D., 78
Blackberry phone: history of, 7; learning management systems of, 45, 60
Blackboard: administration module of, 45; current status of, 60
Blogs, 68, 72, 82
Bloom, B. S., 27
Bloom's taxonomy, 27
Bluetooth, 16
Bozarth, J., 5, 83
Branching scenarios, 69–70
Breadcrumb trails, 67
Brown, J., 21
Brown, J. S., 25
Bruner, J. S., 24
Burns, K., 51
Business simulations, 70
Buttons, 11–12

C

Calculators, 14, 37
Calibre, 59
Cameras, 13, 64
Campus Computing, 2, 60
Capture: description of, 18; examples of, 42–43; importance of, 63; of mobile administrative tasks, 43; practice and, 72–73
Carey, D. O., 24
Carey, L., 24
Carroll, J. M., 96
Carter, D., 52
Cell phones, 1, 84
Channels, 44
Cheating, 64
Civil War (Burns), 51
Clarke, A. C., 3
The cloud, 15

Clues, location, 67
CNET, 41
Code division multiple access (CDMA), 16
Cognition and Technology Group at Vanderbilt, 32
Cognitive apprenticeship framework, 24–25
Cognitive capabilities, 20
Cognitive flexibility theory, 31
Collins, A., 25
Comic strips, 51, 53
Communication capability: as application, 14; description of, 19–20; examples of, 43; of mobile administrative tasks, 43; modes for, 80; for social learning, 78–80; textese in, 84; tools for, 77
Compass, 13
Competency-based performance, 27
Compliance reporting, 66
Compression, 57
Computers: daily use of, 21; students' perception of, 99–100; students' preference for mobile device over, 41; synching mobile devices with, 15
Computing capabilities: description of, 18–19; examples of, 42; of mobile administrative tasks, 43; for performance support, 37
Conative learning, 32
Concepts: definition of, 30; diagrams for presentation of, 53; extension of, 65; media options for, 53; representations of, 31; rote versus models, 30–31
Consistency, 67
Constructivist theory, 24
Content: access to, 58–60; adaptive delivery of, 91–93; customization of, for mobile devices, 52–53; definition of, 49; description of, 17–18; for documents, 56–57; examples of, 42; hosting of, 60; instructional purposes of, 49; introduction to, 33; of media, 49–58; media options for, 54–58; mobile access of, 58–60; of mobile administrative tasks, 43; organizational issues related to, 96–98; sources of, 55–56; web 3.0 and, 91

Farmers, 4

Feedable social media, 81

Feedback, in practice activities, 28, 71, 72

Feltovich, P. J., 25

Files, 49. *See also specific types*

Financial aid, 42

Fixed buttons, 11–12

Flash technology, 17

Flight checklists, 54

Flood simulation, 89

Fonts, 57

Formative assessments, 64

G

Game Boy, 7–8

Games: alternate reality types of, 90–91; for practice interactions, 69, 70; usability goals of, 96

Gery, G., 36

Gick, M. L., 31

Global position systems (GPS): as augmented reality, 87–88; for context-specific content, 54; description of, 12–13

Global system for mobile (GSM), 16

Goals: of learning, 50; of simulation activities, 28, 29

Google, 44–45

Google Docs, 77

Governance, 102

Grammar, 66–67

Grant, W., 3

Granularity, 57, 91

Graphic novels, 51

Graphics, 50, 51

Graphing calculators, 37

Group work, in social learning, 79, 80, 81, 83

GSM. *See* Global system for mobile

H

Haptic mechanisms, 10, 11

Hardware, 98

Hash tags, 68, 80

Health information, 4

Higher education: adaptation of mobile learning by, 2; custom applications created by, 45–46; infrastructure of, 45; mobile-accessible web sites for, 41; response to mobile learning by, 4–5; traditional aim of, 3

Hincke, M., 71

Holeton, R., 3

Holum, A., 25

Holyoak, K. J., 31

Hosting content, 60

HTML, 17, 57

I

IM (instant messaging), 82

Images, compression of, 57

Inert knowledge, 26

Information architecture, 67

Information literacy, 56

Information sharing: for administrative tasks, 42, 43; barriers to, 16; benefits of mobile devices regarding, 10

Information storage, 15

Information technology (IT) departments, 44–46

Infrared Data Association (IrDA), 16

Infrared technology, 16

Input, 11–12

Instant messaging (IM), 82

Institution-specified devices, 101–102

Instructional developers, 98

Intellectricity, 92

Intelligent Tutoring System (ITS) approach, 92

Interaction design: for administrative tasks, 41–42; for practice, 63–73; principles of, 41–44, 66

Interfaces, 11, 66. *See also specific interfaces*

International Telecommunications Union (ITU), 1

Internet: access to, 2, 5; storage on, 15

Introduction, to learning: components of, 24; description of, 33, 53; in learning design, 24; media for, 53, 56

Introspection, 27

Inventory, 13

iOS apps, 60

Ip, A., 81

iPad: growing popularity of, 8; institution-provided, 102; performance support media for, 54; students' preference for, 41

iPhone, 73

iPod: access to content through, 59; history of, 7; input devices of, 12; institution provided, 101

IrDA (Infrared Data Association), 16

IT departments. *See* Information technology departments

ITS (Intelligent Tutoring System) approach, 92

Ittelson, J., 3, 72–73

ITU (International Telecommunications Union), 1

iTunes University, 46, 59

J

Jacobsen, M. J., 25

Jalali, A., 71

Jog dials, 12

Journaling, 65

K

Keller, J., 25, 102

Keyboards, 12

Keypads, 12

Kindle e-reader, 59

Knowledge application. *See* Application, of concepts

Knowledge objectives, 26

K–12 education, 4

Kukulska-Hulme, A., 44

L

Language, of texting, 84

LANs (local area networks), 15–16

Laptop computers, 8, 41

Larkin, J. H., 31

Laurillard, D., 35

Layer, 89

Learner–instructor interactions. *See* Social interactions

Learning: in classrooms versus on mobile devices, 3; goals of, 50, 93–94; importance of understanding, 23; to learn, 33, 36; locus of control

for, 96–97; stages of, 23; traditional order of, 34

Learning design: adaptive delivery in, 91–93; alternate pedagogies in, 33–37; characteristics of, 24–25; concepts in, 30–31; of documents, 56–58; of dynamic content, 58; examples in, 31–32; goal of, 25, 26; introductions in, 33; linear model for, 26–33; media for, 56–68; objectives in, 26–27; organizational issues related to, 95–96; for practice, 63–67; practice in, 27–30; principles of, 41–44; question design in, 69; summaries in, 32

Learning management systems (LMSs): for hosting of content, 60; infrastructure and, 45; organizational issues involving, 97–98; for practice interactions, 66, 69

Learning Studio, 45

Least assistance principle, 96

Lectures: etiquette and, 84; format of, 59–60; media delivery of, 51–52, 59–60

Legal issues, 40

Leigh, E., 81

Levin, J. A. ., 78

Libraries, 42, 43

Lights, 11

Linear model, for learning, 26–33

Linkable social media, 81

Literacy, new types of, 36

Local area networks (LANs), 15–16

Location clues, 67

Location-specific learning: alternate reality in, 89–91; augmented reality in, 87–89; in practice interactions, 71; in social learning, 80–81, 82

Locus of control, 96–97

Long, P. D., 3

M

Mager, R., 27

Manga, 51

Mapping concepts, 31–32

Maps, 43, 54–55

Marketplace, mobile technology, 2

Massachusetts Institute of Technology, 41

Massed practice, 29